Practical. A conversation s
teach you how and when t(
in-law relationships, how to avoid trying to fix your spouse, and
a plethora of other important marriage-related lessons. Through
a series of specific, concise, and thoughtful reflections, you will
inevitably grow in your communication with your spouse. The
format is simple: read, discuss, reflect, and act. You'll love it.

— **Michael Keller**, Lead Pastor, Redeemer Presbyterian
Church, Lincoln Square, New York

In this brief and rich devotional, Steve has given you a set of vir-
tues that can redeem the micro moments that shape the macro
state of your marriage. It is biblical, filled with grace, and highly
practical. Just what you want and need to strengthen the most
important relationship in your life. I would encourage anyone
who wants a revived marriage to read and apply the messages of
this devotional.

— **Tim S. Lane**, President, Institute for Pastoral Care; Author,
Unstuck: A Nine-Step Journey to Change that Lasts

Every couple that walks down the aisle faces marriage conflicts,
but few of us have the resources to resolve them. In this refresh-
ingly honest and uniquely practical devotional, Steve offers us
practical tools for communicating with truth, love, and wisdom.
I recommend reading and working through it at least once a year
with your spouse. It will bring joy, laughter, and the peace of God
to your marriage.

— **Rebekah Lyons**, Author, *Rhythms of Renewal: Trading Stress
and Anxiety for a Life of Peace and Purpose* and *You are Free:
Be Who You Already Are*

Of all the marriage books I've read, this one has swiftly risen to
the top. Writing as both an experienced marriage counselor and

a "marriage practitioner" alongside his lovely wife, Abby, Steve gives valuable wisdom for couples, and from every imaginable angle, to ensure that they can navigate even the hardest parts of marital communication with love. As funny as it sounds, I can't recommend *Marriage Conflict* enough for those who wish to master conflict in their marriages.

—**Scott Sauls**, Senior Pastor, Christ Presbyterian Church, Nashville; Author, *Jesus Outside the Lines* and *A Gentle Answer*

The first sentence of the intro—that's when I wanted in. I knew I would catch a richer vision for Christlike communication with my wife. After having read it, I realize that I have plenty of reasons to ask for forgiveness from her. I've grown up a bit. Hopefully I've become a better husband. Steve's writing is thoughtful, engaging, and biblically rich. My married counselees will love this.

—**Ed Welch**, Counselor and Faculty Member, Christian Counseling and Educational Foundation; Author, *When People Are Big and God Is Small*

MARRIAGE
CONFLICT

31-Day Devotionals for Life

A Series

Deepak Reju
Series Editor

MARRIAGE CONFLICT

TALKING AS TEAMMATES

STEVE HOPPE

P U B L I S H I N G
P.O. BOX 817 • PHILLIPSBURG • NEW JERSEY 08865-0817

This devotional contains several stories and illustrations, many of which come from marriage counseling sessions. All names and identifying details have been changed to preserve anonymity.

Printed in the United States of America

Library of Congress Cataloging-in-Publication Data

Names: Hoppe, Steve, author.
Title: Marriage conflict : talking as teammates / Steve Hoppe.
Description: Phillipsburg, New Jersey : P&R Publishing, 2020. | Series:
  31-day devotionals for life | Summary: "In thirty-one daily readings,
  biblical counselor Steve Hoppe presents a whole new way of communicating
  with your spouse, starting with the heart before moving into the
  practical dos and don'ts"-- Provided by publisher.
Identifiers: LCCN 2019053776 | ISBN 9781629956855 (paperback) | ISBN
  9781629956862 (epub) | ISBN 9781629956879 (mobi)
Subjects: LCSH: Married people--Prayers and devotions. |
  Marriage--Religious aspects--Christianity. | Interpersonal
  communication--Religious aspects--Christianity. | Conflict
  management--Religious aspects--Christianity.
Classification: LCC BV4596.M3 H65 2020 | DDC 242/.644--dc23
LC record available at https://lccn.loc.gov/2019053776

To my best friend, Abby

Contents

A Word to Couples Reading This Book Together

A STRUGGLING COUPLE decides to take a much-needed Caribbean vacation to rest, relax, and revive their marriage. On the second day, they go scuba diving. As they explore the wonder of God's underwater creation, they see a small wooden box partially covered by a mound of sand on the ocean floor. They dig it up, haul it back to the boat, and open it. To their amazement, it's filled with gold coins. They've found a bona fide treasure chest!

The devotional in your hands is like this couples' treasure chest, only better. It is filled not with *material* riches but with *spiritual* riches. Steve has written a power-packed, heart-convicting, Scripture-saturated, hope-filled devotional for any husband and wife wanting to transform the way that they engage in conflict. By starting with the heart and working outward, this book helps couples

- who are newly married and lack the skills they need to tackle the trials of marriage,
- who have been together for years but have never learned how to communicate well,
- who are living in verbal war zones,
- who want a clear list of dos and don'ts when conflict arises,
- who are discouraged and don't know where else to turn,
- who want to take a "pretty good" marriage and make it stronger,
- who want to train other couples to lovingly engage in conflict,
- who are marriage counselors,
- who need marriage counseling,
- who are not yet married but want to thrive once they do tie the knot,

- who love Jesus and simply want to speak to others in a way that honors him.

If any of these descriptors fit you, then turn the page and start reading. Work through this devotional, day by day, for the coming month.

The beauty of this devotional is that each day offers stand-alone wisdom—individual gold coins—for working through marriage conflict. As you skimmed through the table of contents, I trust that some days stood out more than others. Maybe the two of you are particularly prone to avoiding conflict, exaggerating, or overly correcting each other, for example. After working through the whole devotional, go back to these particular readings and work through them a few more times. You will want to absorb the wisdom, grace, and truth in them.

You don't need to look for a hidden treasure to find riches for your marriage. This devotional is the treasure that you need. Riches abound in its pages. I promise that you'll be blessed, encouraged, and challenged by it. I was. And every couple I've given this devotional to has come back stronger in their communication and more rooted in their faith.

That's enough from me. Now it's time to let Steve speak for himself. Let's begin.

Deepak Reju

INTRODUCTION

A Matter of Life and Death

"YOU'RE GONNA BURN IN HELL for what you just said. You're a LIAR. You're a HYPOCRITE. You're TRASH, and you'll ALWAYS BE TRASH."

John shouted these words at his wife Melissa at the tail end of our last marriage counseling session together. He violently slapped the couch, pointed his finger in her face, and stomped his foot as he screamed. When he finished his tirade, he stormed out of the room, slammed the door, and left the building. Without his wife.

That same week I counseled Bill and Sarah—a struggling yet softhearted couple. During the middle of our session, things started getting heated. In an effort to change the relational temperature of the room, I paused the conversation and asked a question: "What do you love about each other?"

Bill looked at me with cynical eyes. He went along with the exercise anyway. "Well . . . [long pause] . . . she's beautiful, she's kind . . ."

I stopped him. "No, say it *to her*. And dig deep. No trite clichés. Go."

He turned and faced Sarah, looked into her eyes, and spoke from his heart.

"You're beautiful. But you're not only physically beautiful—your *soul* is beautiful. You genuinely care about people—your family, your friends, strangers at Starbucks . . . *everybody*. You're a reflection of Jesus—a far better one than I am. You're a passionate and patient mom. You tirelessly take care of our home. You push me to work hard, encourage me when I succeed, and consistently point me to Christ. In the end, you make me a better person. You're my best friend. I love you."

A tear trickled down Sarah's cheek.

Next it was her turn. She collected herself, turned to Bill, and spoke.

"Bill, you're a man after God's own heart. You love him more than anything else in the world. Your character shows it. You're a selfless husband and a far better parent than I am. You endlessly sacrifice for our children. You help them with their homework. You coach their sports teams. You take time every day to teach them about Jesus. You do way more than my father ever did for me. Plus, you're humble, gentle, and funny. You make me laugh constantly. You're my best friend. I love you."

A matching tear fell down Bill's cheek.

Two couples. Two radically different communication dynamics.

In the first scene, John was murdering Melissa.

Wait, *murdering*?

Yes. He was metaphorically killing her. Proverbs 18:21 says that "death and life are in the power of the tongue." This means that our words have the power to figuratively slay our spouses or rejuvenate their souls. John was doing the former. He was tearing out Melissa's heart and leaving her in my counseling office to die.

Bill and Sarah, however, were doing the latter. They were offering each other life. Their words were encouraging, edifying, and energizing. After our little exercise, their hearts were revived— beating harder for each other and, more importantly, for Christ.

Sadly, like John and Melissa, when we engage in conflict as married couples, many of us are slowly killing each other with our words rather than infusing life. Abby and I were certainly guilty of this during our first five years of marriage. We interrupted, insulted, and intentionally irritated each other. We were experts at boasting, belittling, and blame-shifting. We focused on the specks in each other's eyes and ignored the logs in our own (Matt. 7:3–5). We murdered each other over and over again with our words.

But at the half-decade mark, we turned a corner. Thanks to a season of robust self-reflection, radical repentance, and regular marriage counseling (thanks, Ed Welch), we threw down our weapons and began talking as teammates instead of opponents. Our words lost their biting edge. We started listening with intention, complimenting with sincerity, and pointing each other to Jesus as we spoke. We made the decision to offer life—not death—with our words.

My hope is that you will experience a similar shift in your marriage as you read this devotional. I want you to communicate through conflict in a way that will breathe life into each other's hearts. I want you to throw down your weapons and become God's messengers to each other. Spirit-filled messengers.

I want your *entire relationship* to change.

The format of this devotional is straightforward. It consists of thirty-one daily readings containing the following three components:

- a short Bible passage
- a discussion of how the passage addresses a topic related to communication and conflict resolution in marriage
- a set of questions and exercises to spur contemplation and conversation

The goal is to take one month to read this devotional together. Get separate copies. Take notes in the margins. Dig deep into the material on your own and then dig deep together. Think. Meditate. Pray as you read. Talk regularly about what you're reading. Consider holding semi-regular date nights to discuss the readings. Challenge each other. Don't pretend to have it all together. Be honest about yourself and your marriage. You won't benefit from this book unless you're willing to get real.

What if your spouse is unwilling to join you in reading this devotional? Should you read it anyway? Absolutely. You can't control anybody but yourself. And God wants you to handle conflict with your spouse in a healthy and holy manner.

What if you are not a Christian? What if you don't believe in God? What if you think that the Bible is just a piece of historical fiction? Should you still read this devotional? Once again, yes. I trust that your marriage will still benefit tremendously if you dive into its content and apply its principles.

But this devotional isn't for everybody. Who is it *not* for?

- *A spouse looking for quick fixes.* The purpose of this book is not to provide you with rapid-fire solutions to all your unique marriage problems. Instead, its purpose is to teach you gospel-centered principles to help you navigate through these problems in productive and life-giving ways.
- *A spouse playing the blame game.* If you're reading this devotional to prove that your spouse is the reason for your marriage struggles, this devotional isn't for you. The goal here is to work on you, your relationship with God, and your relationship with your spouse—not to shine a spotlight on your spouse's sins and shortcomings.
- *A spouse committed to isolation.* Marriage is meant to be lived out in the context of community—specifically the community of your local church. You will need trusted brothers and sisters in Christ to hold you accountable, encourage you, and challenge you as you work through this devotional. If you want to isolate yourself, this book isn't for you.
- *A spouse being abused.* If you are being abused by your spouse, your first priorities should include removing yourself from the abusive situation, telling the proper authorities, and getting the help that you need. This devotional can wait.

Who, then, is this devotional for?
Everybody else.

Your marriage is the most important human relationship in your life. The stakes are high. You have the ability to carry your spouse to the top of the world or to drive them into the ground with your words. With that said, I can't think of a better way to get started than by praying for both of you as you learn how to communicate together in the midst of conflict in a gracious and God-glorifying manner . . .

> Lord Jesus, may you bless this couple as they read this devotional together. May it lead them to experience healthy and holy communication during the challenging times of marriage. May you draw them closer to each other and closer to you over these thirty-one days. And may you receive all the glory, honor, and praise as you do this.
>
> In Jesus's name I pray. Amen.

MARRIAGE CONFLICT
STARTING POINTS

DAY 1

Dig to the Root

"For out of the abundance of the heart the mouth speaks." (Matt. 12:34)

"We hate each other."

When I asked Bob and Susan what brought them to counseling, this was their response. They were twelve years into their marriage and had been fighting ruthlessly for the last two. Susan referred to them as "ticking time bombs ready to explode." Their anger had escalated to the point that they were ready to file for divorce. They needed help. Stat.

After one session with the couple, however, I realized that anger wasn't the root of their problem. It was just a symptom. We needed to dig deeper into their hearts if we were going to save their marriage.

Jesus tells us why. In Matthew 12:34, he says that "out of the abundance of the heart the mouth speaks." In Matthew 15:19, he says that our thoughts and actions also flow from our hearts. If we are going to change the way that we relate to our spouses, we must start there. We must do the hard work of *heart* work. We must uncover the lies that we believe about God, ourselves, the world, and the devil. We must identify the idols that we are worshipping—the things, people, and feelings that we are functionally elevating above God in value, importance, power, and authority over our lives. We must unearth the sins underneath our sins. We must dig to the roots if we are going to change the fruit.

What was at the root of Bob and Susan's anger? Pride.

I'll start with Susan. Two years prior, Bob had lost his job as a high-level Wall Street executive. When he lost his job, Susan lost something as well. She lost face. She lost the ability to impress her Manhattan friends with her husband's growing list of professional accomplishments. She lost the opportunity to wow people with the expensive clothes, jewelry, and purses that his old salary had afforded her. She lost her identity as the wife of a corporate superstar. Her ego was deflated, and her rage was her way of punishing Bob for metaphorically letting the air out.

Bob's anger was also rooted in pride. Growing up, he wasn't popular. He wasn't good-looking. He didn't have girlfriends. He didn't have guy friends. He was a nobody. But when he graduated from college and entered the business world, everything changed. His exceptional intelligence and business savvy propelled him up the corporate ladder. People started paying attention to him. He had status and dignity. His career gave him pride. When he lost his job, he lost this pride. In his eyes, he was a nobody once again. This made him angry, and he was taking his anger out on Susan.

Bob and Susan had hearts rooted in pride. That's why they were angry.

Where is *your* heart rooted?

Reflect as a Couple: Have the two of you been using surface-level treatments to address your marriage problems instead of digging into the unhealthy heart conditions underneath them?

Reflect by Yourself: Recall your most recent fight with your spouse. What in your heart was driving your unholy words or behaviors?

Act: When marriage conflict arises and our hearts are rooted in anything but Jesus, we are doomed. Hatred replaces love. Anger replaces compassion. Harshness replaces gentleness. And the list goes on. Confess to each other how you have been rooting your hearts in things other than Christ. Pray together that he would take your hearts and root them in himself.

DAY 2

Check Your Tone

But the fruit of the Spirit is love, joy, peace, patience,
kindness, goodness, faithfulness, gentleness, self-control;
against such things there is no law. (Gal. 5:22–23)

"LISTEN, MEREDITH . . . I'm sorry. I'm a bad husband and a bad father. I work too much. I travel too much. I don't spend enough time with the kids. I don't spend enough time with your family. I slack on chores. I don't give you the attention that you deserve. I'm really sorry."

After six years of a roller-coaster marriage and three months of separation, this was Scott's apology to his wife. Seems like a decent one, right?

Now read it again, but imagine Scott's tone as angry, agitated, and annoyed—lacking a hint of true regret, remorse, or repentance. Imagine that he wasn't really sorry. Imagine him apologizing only to avoid being a middle-aged divorcee and a weekend-only dad. That's how he sounded. His words said "Sorry." His tone said "Not sorry." And he couldn't mask it.

Not surprisingly, Meredith wasn't fooled. She called his bluff. And when she did, he predictably exploded on her in a fit of rage.

In yesterday's devotional, we learned that our words flow from our hearts. But the story of Meredith and Scott shows that the *tone* of our words also flows from our hearts—and our tone can be just as deadly or life-giving as our words. Sweet words coupled with a harsh tone can kill. Challenging words coupled with a gentle tone can bring life.

How can your tone become holy? You must be filled with the Holy Spirit. If you are filled with the Spirit, your speech will be laced with love, joy, peace, patience, kindness, goodness, faithfulness, gentleness, and self-control (Gal. 5:22–23). Out of the abundance of your heart you will speak Christlike, Spirit-filled, fruitful words. You will sound like Jesus.

How do you know if your tone is holy? How can you be sure that your words sound Christlike? Don't ask yourself. Why not? You're probably tone-deaf. Scott certainly was. He thought that he sounded gentle and sincere. He didn't. He sounded bitter because in his heart he *was* bitter. So instead of asking *yourself* if your tone is holy, ask two other people. First, ask your spouse. Trust me— they can hear your tone with crystal clarity. Second, ask God. Ask him to shine a light on your heart to expose any impurity that is causing you to speak with an unloving tone.

Words matter. But tone matters too.

Maybe more.

> **Reflect as a Couple:** What are the most common ungodly tones that you hear in each other's voices? Tones of condescension? Mockery? Irritation? Impatience? Anger? Passive aggressiveness? How do these tones make you feel when you are on the receiving end?
>
> **Reflect by Yourself:** Which specific fruits of the Spirit do you typically lack when you speak to your spouse in the midst of conflict? Will you pray for them right now?
>
> **Act:** When conflict arises and you verbally wound each other, confess to each other both your hurtful words *and your hurtful tones.* Ask for forgiveness from each other and from God. Trust that, if you are Christians, you are forgiven by God because of Christ's death on the cross (1 John 1:9).

DAY 3

Hydrate Frequently

*Jesus answered her, "If you knew the gift of God, and who it is
that is saying to you, 'Give me a drink,' you would have asked
him, and he would have given you living water." (John 4:10)*

"YOU NEED TO go do a quiet time, Steve."

This gentle rebuke from Abby means that I need to spend
time with God because I'm worshipping some idol, believing
some lie, or telling myself some godless narrative and as a result
speaking to her like a self-righteous jerk. In other words, my heart
is as hard as a rock and needs hydration ASAP.

What form of hydration does it need? Living water. What's
that? We find out in the gospel of John. Jesus introduces this
enigmatic beverage when he strikes up a conversation with a
Samaritan woman at a well and asks her for a drink. With Jews
and Samaritans being relative enemies at the time, she's caught off
guard by his request. She asks him, "How is it that you, a Jew, ask
for a drink from me, a woman of Samaria?" (John 4:9). Instead
of answering her question directly, Jesus shifts the conversation
away from physical water and offers her living water. Later on, we
discover that this living water is the life-giving, soul-satisfying,
thirst-quenching Holy Spirit given to all who place their faith in
Christ (John 7:38–39).

We must hydrate ourselves with living water—we must be
filled with the Holy Spirit—if our communication is to produce
life instead of death when we are in marriage conflict. But how
do we drink living water? What practical steps can we take to be
filled with the Spirit? Here is a list of things that you can do as a
couple to drink living water together:

- Read and discuss the Bible.
- Pray daily.
- Spend Christ-focused time with other Christians.
- Attend and volunteer in a solid Bible-teaching church.
- Serve your community outside the church.
- Partake in the sacraments of baptism and the Lord's Supper.
- Talk about Jesus with those who don't share your beliefs.
- Give generously.

The more living water you consume, the healthier the roots of your heart will be. And the holier your communication will be when conflict arises.

Reflect as a Couple: Are you drinking living water as individuals and as a couple? Is your communication thriving in the midst of conflict as a result? Or are you functionally rejecting Christ by refusing to drink this water? How is this negatively impacting your communication?

Reflect by Yourself: What in your heart is keeping you from drinking living water with your spouse? Busyness? Laziness? Fear? Discomfort? Something else?

Act: Based on today's bulleted list of ways to regularly drink living water as a couple, develop a robust plan of how you will do so moving forward. Get as practical as possible.

MARRIAGE CONFLICT
PITFALLS

DAY 4

Avoiding Conflict

As iron sharpens iron, so one person sharpens another. (Prov. 27:17 NIV)

"I GO OUT of my way to avoid conflict with my partner."

It's one of over two hundred statements on an assessment that I administer to couples to evaluate their matrimonial health. Potential responses range on a scale from "strongly disagree" to "strongly agree." I've found that the most common response is "strongly agree." In other words, couples *love* avoiding conflict.

This is bad for at least three reasons.

First, conflict avoidance is typically rooted in idolatry. If you're consciously fleeing marriage conflict, it's usually because you're worshipping a false god. Take Mark as an example. When he would critique his wife Emily during their first few years of marriage, she would instinctively criticize him back—often to a harsher degree. She would raise her voice, call him names, and manipulate the conversation to make everything his fault. Things would rapidly spiral out of control, leaving him agitated, anxious, and upset. To avoid feeling this way, he stopped correcting her. When she sinned against him, he would shut his mouth and put a smile on his face. He chose serenity over her sanctification and harmony over her holiness. He avoided conflict with Emily because he was worshipping the idol of peace.

Second, conflict avoidance is bad because God uses conflict to sharpen us—to make us more like Christ. Proverbs 27:17 (NIV) says, "As iron sharpens iron, so one person sharpens another." How does a metalworker use iron to sharpen iron? First, he heats a dull, jagged piece until it becomes ductile. He then takes a cold, sharp piece and uses it to cut a straight line along the molten piece's edge to eliminate its surface irregularities. When the molten piece cools, it has a brand-new sharp edge. In a similar way, our skilled metalworker (God) uses intense heat (marriage conflict) to "melt" us. He then takes a cold, knifelike piece of iron (our spouses) and, through a process of calculated cutting (confrontation and admonishment), sharpens (sanctifies) us. When we avoid conflict, we miss out on being sharpened by our spouses and by God.

Finally, conflict avoidance is bad because it contradicts the conflict-saturated life and ministry of Christ. Jesus confronted sin (John 2:13–16). He challenged hypocrisy and wrong belief among influential religious leaders (Matt. 23). He even said to his good friend Peter, "Get behind me, Satan!" (Matt. 16:23). Ultimately, he faced the conflict of the crucifixion and willfully endured it to obey his Father and save his followers. He entered conflict out of love for God and love for others.

Will you do the same in your marriage?

Reflect as a Couple: Are there conversation topics that are off-limits in your marriage because they stir up too much conflict? Will you prayerfully consider talking about these topics—perhaps with a wise counselor, pastor, or couple from your local church to help guide the conversation and make it constructive?

Reflect by Yourself: The call to enter into conflict doesn't give you license to be aggressive or combative as you do so. How might God be calling you to adjust your posture, tone, and speech so your spouse feels safe and loved when you engage in conflict?

Act: Is idolatry causing either of you to avoid conflict? Take time together to reflect, pray, and openly repent of such idolatry before God. Then faithfully and lovingly move toward each other and enter into the difficult conversations that you've been avoiding.

DAY 5

Fighting

*"You have heard that it was said, 'You shall love your neighbor
and hate your enemy.' But I say to you, Love your enemies
and pray for those who persecute you." (Matt. 5:43–44)*

"WE WANT TO learn how to fight fair."

When I started marriage counseling with Sharon and Tom,
this was their goal. For years, when conflict would surface, they
would put on figurative boxing gloves and attack each other. They
would jab at each other's insecurities. They would hit each other
below the belt with bruising insults and violent name-calling.
They would take shots at each other's friends, families, and faith.
They would use any verbal fighting tactic necessary to knock the
other person out.

They entered my office that day bleeding. Each spouse had
caused irreparable emotional damage—apparently from fighting unfairly. They wanted me to teach them how to "fight fair" to
minimize such damage.

I told them I wouldn't do it.

Why not? Because fighting has no place in marriage—even
if it's "fair." Fighting, by definition, pits two enemies against each
other—each trying to defeat the other. But in marriage you aren't
enemies. You're *teammates*. In fact, you're such close teammates
that God mysteriously refers to you as "one flesh" (Gen. 2:24).
You joined this two-person, one-flesh team when you signed your
marriage covenant on your wedding day. You will hopefully stay
on this team until the day you die.

And even if your spouse feels like your enemy, Jesus doesn't
allow fighting. Instead, in Matthew 5:43–44, he demands that you
show your "enemy" love. This means laying down your life for

your spouse instead of insisting on your own way. It means pouring out patience instead of agitation. It means being kind instead of rude, humble instead of arrogant, selfless instead of selfish, and forgiving instead of resentful. And as if this weren't enough, Jesus also wants you to *pray* for your spouse. He wants you to ask God to bless your spouse.

This is no small task. If you rely on your willpower, you will fail. When tensions flare, you will slap on the gloves and fight your spouse. Where do you find the strength to show love when your spouse feels like an enemy? You must turn to the one who loved us while we were *his* enemies (Rom. 5:10). You must ask for strength from the one who destroyed the greatest enemy that was facing you and me—death itself (1 Cor. 15:26). You must kneel before Jesus Christ—the one who became the Father's enemy on the cross to save you from hell—and beg him to fill you with so much love that it overflows all over your spouse.

Fighting isn't allowed in marriage. When your spouse feels like your enemy, Jesus gives you only one option: love.

Reflect as a Couple: Do you see each other as enemies? You aren't. How should your status as one-flesh teammates change the way that you engage in conflict?

Reflect by Yourself: When you fight with your spouse, what are you *really* fighting for? Approval? Control? Respect? Something else?

Act: The next time things are getting heated between the two of you, press the pause button and take a time-out (see Day 27 for more on this). Go for walks by yourselves. On your walks, take off your boxing gloves and remind yourselves that you are on the same team. Pray for each other. Pray for yourselves. When you both return, show each other love—not hatred.

DAY 6

Checking Out

And the Word became flesh and dwelt among us, and
we have seen his glory, glory as of the only Son from the
Father, full of grace and truth. (John 1:14)

A SHELL.

This was how Catherine and David described their marriage of five years. Things looked beautiful on the outside. They were experts at putting on happy faces in front of their friends, family, and church. But behind closed doors, their relationship was hollow. They didn't eat, sleep, pray, or even talk together. They were functional roommates at best.

How did their marriage become a shell? The answer goes back to their first year of marriage. During this adjustment year, they fought relentlessly over finances, sex, paint colors, weekend plans . . . you name it. Things were a mess. But as Christians, they knew that they didn't have grounds to divorce. So they implemented a coping strategy. They checked out. They escaped their marriage conflict by escaping their marriage altogether. David upped his work hours, joined two basketball leagues, and built a man cave in his basement. Catherine got a second job selling essential oils, filled her social calendar to the brim, and holed up in her (separate) bedroom when she was at home. David and Catherine weren't only avoiding conflict—they were avoiding each other.

Many of us do the same when marriage conflict arises. We check out. We escape to places where our marriage problems don't exist. Some of us binge-watch TV shows. Some of us work obsessively. Some of us turn to alcohol, drugs, or pornography. When things get tough, we run away from our spouses instead of running toward them in love.

But in John 1:14, we read about one who did the opposite. In the incarnation, Jesus Christ left heaven, took on flesh, and "checked in" to our conflict-filled world to pursue his bride, the church. Even when she doubted him (John 20:24–29), denied him (Mark 14:66–72), and deserted him (Matt. 26:56), he never stopped pursuing her. He committed himself to the Father's will and stayed checked in until his last breath on the cross.

And he remains checked in today. Even when we temporarily check out of our relationship with Jesus, he still earnestly pursues us. He stays with us (Matt. 28:20), purifies us (Phil. 1:6), protects us (John 10:28), prays for us (Rom. 8:34), and never stops loving us (Rom. 8:38–39). He never leaves us or forsakes us (Heb. 13:5). He remains checked in. Always.

Will you do the same in your marriage when conflict arises? Will you remain checked in? Will you fight the urge to give up and withdraw to places, activities, work, or people (your children included) when times are tough? Will you immerse yourself in difficult and uncomfortable conversations when you *really* want to avoid them? Will you resist the urge to check out?

Reflect as a Couple: Have either of you checked out of your marriage?

Reflect by Yourself: Mentally fantasizing about a life without your spouse is one way to check out of your marriage. Do you do this? If so, will you put such fantasies to rest?

Act: As a way of modeling the incarnational ministry of Jesus, consider holding weekly "check-ins" in which you dive into each other's lives, ask questions, expose your hearts, and pray together.

DAY 7

Fixing

"And I will give you a new heart, and a new spirit I will put within you. And I will remove the heart of stone from your flesh and give you a heart of flesh. And I will put my Spirit within you, and cause you to walk in my statutes and be careful to obey my rules." (Ezek. 36:26–27)

IN MY EARLY TWENTIES, I somehow landed a job as an engineer with NASA at the Johnson Space Center. It was my dream job. I sat in meetings with astronauts on a daily basis. I worked with some of the smartest scientific minds on the planet. I was a part of the team that sent the first robot into outer space. I had to pinch myself every day as I pulled up to work.

But the best part of working at NASA was that I was being paid to do something that I loved—*fix things*. I got to play with broken gadgets and restore them to life. I got to analyze faulty mechanical systems and get them operating smoothly again. I got to study glitch-filled computer programs and recode them so they ran properly. I was a problem solver. I got to fix things. All day long.

It was terrible training for marriage.

Why? Because my job as Abby's husband isn't to fix her.

When marriage conflict arises and our spouses' sins and shortcomings surface, many of us enter "fix it" mode. We offer unhelpful correction, criticism, and counsel in an effort to change our spouses—to conform them into the spouses *we* think they should be.

But fixing our spouses isn't our job. It's God's. He alone can fix any of us. How does he do it? He reengineers our hearts. Ezekiel 36:26–27 describes the process—one that applies to all Christians. It starts with him removing our spiritually dead hearts of stone and replacing them with spiritually alive hearts of flesh—a process called *regeneration*. He then fills us with his Spirit and spends the rest of our lives continuously molding our new hearts into ones that produce Christlike thoughts, words, and actions (Phil. 1:6; Heb. 9:14). He programs us so we "walk in his statutes" and "obey his rules."

God is the divine engineer in charge of fixing your spouse. You aren't.

Why might you try to fix your spouse when you are in a conflict? Perhaps the reason is pride—you think you *can* do it. Perhaps it's functional unbelief—you don't think that God can do it. Perhaps it's impatience—you don't want to wait for God to do it. Perhaps it's idolatry—you're worshipping the idol of control.

No matter the reason, when conflict arises and sin abounds, you don't need to fix your spouse. You need to love your spouse. Sure, this might mean offering a gentle correction or a soft rebuke. But it doesn't mean playing the Holy Spirit and trying to meticulously micromanage them into a state of greater holiness.

The next time that you're in a conflict and you see sin in your spouse's heart, will you relinquish control and allow God to do the fixing?

He's much better at it.

Reflect as a Couple: In what ways are you trying to fix each other?

Reflect by Yourself: What is at the heart of your attempts to fix your spouse? Pride? Functional unbelief? Impatience? Idolatry? All of the above? Something else?

Act: Confess to each other the ways that you've been trying to play the Holy Spirit when you've been in conflict. Ask for forgiveness for trying to fix each other.

DAY 8

Exaggerating

"You shall not bear false witness against your neighbor." (Exod. 20:16)

"You're always angry." "You *constantly* belittle me." "I'm your *last* priority." "You *never* want to go on dates." "I do *everything* for the family." Danielle slammed Luke with these five complaints in a single fifty-minute marriage counseling session. Their common denominator? Exaggeration. With each complaint, Danielle grossly overstated the scope of Luke's behavior.

Exaggeration has no place in healthy marriage conflict for at least two reasons. First, it's a form of lying—a breach of the ninth commandment (Exod. 20:16). It takes something that is true, stretches it, and turns it into something that is untrue. Paul tells us that instead of exaggerating, we must "speak the truth in love" (Eph. 4:15). We must use language that is both true and transformative. Our words should be saturated with integrity as they encourage, edify, educate, and energize our spouses.

Second, exaggerations come across as character assassinations—assaults on who our spouses *are*, not on what they've just done. Here are three examples: (1) Chad forgets to take out the trash. Mary tells him that he's *always* forgetful. Chad hears that he's an absentminded idiot. (2) Stacy asks Dan to drive slower in the grocery store parking lot. Dan complains that she's *constantly* criticizing him. Stacy hears that she's a condescending nag. (3) Rick is ten minutes late to dinner. Tara tells him that he's *never* on time. Rick hears that he's an irresponsible moron. The point is that an exaggeration moves beyond the action and attacks the person at their core.

Here are three ways to avoid exaggerating when you're in the midst of a conflict:

1. Talk concretely about what just happened or what is currently happening instead of making sweeping generalizations rooted in the past.

2. Barring exceptional circumstances, eliminate the following words from your vocabulary when you're critiquing your spouse: *always, never, all, none, everything, nothing, everybody, nobody, constantly, completely, entirely,* and *thoroughly.* There are several others, but you get the gist of it.

3. If you notice a trend of negative behavior in your spouse, gently identify the trend without exaggerating. Make sure to cite specific examples. If you think that there is a trend but you lack examples, it might be best to start logging instances of the behavior—not to hold them over your spouse but rather to verify the trend that you see.

Exaggeration is hurtful. It's a form of lying. It feels like character assassination. It's time to cut it out of your marriage.

Reflect as a Couple: Is exaggeration common in your conversations together?

Reflect by Yourself: Why do you exaggerate? What are you hoping to accomplish?

Act: It's hard to break the habit of exaggerating. But if you do so, you will become more like Christ. In him there is no lying—no exaggeration. He was and is the essence of *truth* (John 14:6). Commit together to emulate the character of Christ and to eliminate exaggeration from your speech. Pray that the Holy Spirit would help you to do so.

DAY 9

Swearing

*But now you must put them all away: anger, wrath, malice,
slander, and obscene talk from your mouth. (Col. 3:8)*

Why lies He in such mean estate,
Where ox and ass are feeding?

If you don't recognize these words, they begin the second
stanza of the Christmas hymn "What Child is This?" If you're
like me, you cringe every time you sing them. Particularly
because of the eleventh word. While the hymn's composer, William
Dix, used the word to refer to a donkey, it has become a
contemporary swear word. And worship and swear words don't
go together.

Along the same lines, if a Christian marriage is meant to be a
continual act of worship, swearing doesn't belong in it either.

Paul denounces swearing in Colossians 3:8, where he tells
Christians to eliminate "obscene talk" from their mouths. The
command comes in the middle of his description of how to put
away our "old selves" and take on "new selves." If we are to become
new, holy selves, we must fixate our focus on heavenly things
(vv. 1–2), run from immorality and idolatry (vv. 5–7), annihilate
anger (v. 8), destroy deception (v. 9), conform our character
into that of Christ (v. 10), and love others lavishly (vv. 12–17). In
other words, as new selves we must live lives of continuous worship.
Hence why swearing—"obscene talk"—doesn't belong.

What does swearing do in a Christian marriage?

- *It hurts you.* Swear words are like drugs. They feel good in the
  moment. They're highly addictive. You develop a tolerance to
  them as you use them more and more. Eventually, you can't

stop using them, and a relational chasm is created between you and God.

- *It hurts your spouse.* Swearing in the home creates a toxic verbal environment for your spouse. Swearing *at* your spouse fires lethal verbal darts into their heart.
- *It hurts others.* If you and your spouse swear inside your marriage, you will swear outside of your marriage. I guarantee it. Doing so could cause other Christians to stumble (Mark 9:42). It could push those who aren't Christians further away from Jesus (Matt. 23:13). It could severely limit your influence in the kingdom of God (James 1:26).
- *It hurts God.* Using swear words takes wonderful things created by God—human body parts, intimate acts between a husband and a wife, you name it—and adds to them an undertone of evil. This brings God sadness and anger instead of the glory that he is due.

In the end, Paul tells us that every word we speak to our spouses should build them up (Eph. 4:29). I've never heard swear words do this. Let's eliminate them.

Reflect as a Couple: Have you allowed swearing to rear its ugly head in times of conflict with each other?

Reflect by Yourself: What are the underlying heart conditions that lead you to swear?

Act: Jesus Christ—the only one whose mouth was perfectly pure—died to forgive you of your impure mouth. Out of gratitude for what he has done for you, commit to eliminating obscene talk. Replace it with talk that honors God and breathes life into your marriage.

DAY 10

Catastrophizing

He who began a good work in you will carry it on to
completion until the day of Christ Jesus. (Phil. 1:6 NIV)

ADAM FORGETS TO take out the dog. His wife Jenny says, "We shouldn't have kids because I know I'll be doing all the work."

Kelly screams violently at Zack. Zack whispers under his breath, "Great, I'm going to be in a verbally abusive marriage for the rest of my life."

Todd leaves the toilet seat up. Amanda yells, "Put the seat down, Todd! I'm not going to be your wife *and* mother for the next fifty years!"

Jenny, Zack, and Amanda are committing a common marriage foul: catastrophizing. To catastrophize is to take a single event or behavioral trend and project that it will never end—potentially escalating in magnitude and resulting in cataclysmic disaster. In marriage, we catastrophize when we assume that our spouses' sins, vices, or mistakes will continue indefinitely and that our lives and marriages will be horrific as a result.

What's at the heart of catastrophizing? You are functionally believing either that God *can't* change your spouse, or, if you know that he can, that he *won't* change your spouse.

In other words, you're believing lies. Here's the truth: if God created the universe, parted the Red Sea, sent down manna from heaven, delivered Jonah from the belly of an enormous fish, and raised Christ from the dead, he can change your spouse. If God changed Paul—a killer of Christians—he can change your spouse. If God changed you, he can change your spouse. And if your spouse is a Christian, Paul says in Philippians 1:6 that the Lord—the one who replaced your spouse's heart of stone with a heart of flesh—*will* continue to purify this heart until the day that Jesus returns. He *will* change your spouse.

Instead of catastrophizing when your spouse fails, let me encourage you to do three things:

1. *Pray.* Ask the Lord to change your spouse. He's the only one with the ability to do it. Specifically plead that God would perform heart surgery on your spouse and root out the core issues underlying their behavior.
2. *Trust.* Believe that God is true to his Word and will complete the good work that he began in your spouse.
3. *Pray for patience.* God doesn't promise *when* he will change your spouse—only that he *will* change your spouse.

Catastrophizing is hurtful. But worse than this, it's blasphemous. It denies the reality of who God is and what he says he'll do with all his children. Let's put an end to it.

Reflect as a Couple: Do you believe God's promise that he will purify you and your spouse and continue doing so until the day Christ returns? How should this change the way that you speak to each other?

Reflect by Yourself: How have you catastrophized in your marriage? In what areas have you lost hope that your spouse will change? Where can you find hope?

Act: When your spouse blows it, stay in the moment. Take your thoughts captive (2 Cor. 10:5) and battle the temptation to project your present reality into the distant future.

40

DAY 11

Comparing

*"You shall not covet your neighbor's wife, or his male
servant, or his female servant, or his ox, or his donkey, or
anything that is your neighbor's." (Exod. 20:17)*

I've PERMANENTLY DELETED Facebook from my phone.
No, there isn't anything inherently wrong with the app. I've
deleted it because it tempts me to compare myself with others.
When I scroll through the pictures, anecdotes, and status updates
of friends and strangers, I place one eye on their lives and one eye
on mine. And I fall into a trap. I become covetous.

I see the lives of others—often embellished fairy-tale versions of their lives—and I desperately want to be them. I want to
have what they have, look how they look, and succeed as they've
succeeded. I suspect I'm not alone here. Comparison almost uni-
versally breeds feelings of covetousness—a toxic and sinful emo-
tion (Exod. 20:17).

If you are in the midst of marriage conflict, you will be
tempted to play two versions of the comparison game.

Version 1: Comparing your marriage to other marriages. If
you do this when you're in conflict, your marriage will almost
certainly fall short. After all, you're in conflict! You will long for
the unrealistically polished marriages that people present pub-
licly—marriages that don't really exist. And you will be coveting.

Version 2: Comparing your spouse to other spouses. When
you're in conflict, it will also be tempting to compare your
spouse to other married men or women. When your spouse
inevitably falls short (again, you're in conflict), you will want
one of the "better" spouses out there, and, once again, you will
be coveting.

How do you avoid covetousness in marriage? Here are three tips:

1. *Practice the discipline of gratitude.* Your loving Father sovereignly ordained that you would be married to your spouse. Thank him for your marriage. Praise him for blessing you with your spouse.
2. *Pray for your spouse.* As you earnestly intercede on your spouse's behalf, your mind will stop focusing on other couples, and your heart will attach to your spouse in new and holy ways (Matt. 6:21).
3. *Find contentment in Jesus.* Your spouse will never make you content. As Paul says in Philippians 4:11–13, the secret to having contentment is to find it in Christ. Pray that your heart would be so satisfied in Jesus that it wouldn't need to be satisfied by your spouse.

I've heard it said that comparison is the thief of joy. Be joyful. And stop playing the comparison game.

Reflect as a Couple: Is comparison stealing your joy as a couple?

Reflect by Yourself: Are there people to whom you have compared your spouse during hard times? Have you wounded your spouse by verbalizing these comparisons? Will you repent right now and stop playing the comparison game?

Act: The only spouse who will never fall short is Jesus Christ. Instead of leaving you disillusioned and covetous, he will leave you astonished and satisfied. When you are tempted to compare your marriage and your spouse to other marriages and spouses, go vertical and reflect on the beauty and wonder of your heavenly spouse. Instead of foolishly trying to find contentment in your earthly spouse, find it in Christ.

DAY 12

Typing instead of Talking

*"If your brother sins against you, go and tell him his
fault, between you and him alone. If he listens to you,
you have gained your brother." (Matt. 18:15)*

"YOU DIDN'T MAKE the bed before you left for work."

Greg received this brief text message from his wife Adrienne
on a Monday afternoon. The previous Saturday, they had talked
at length about chore division in the home. Greg had committed to tidy up their bedroom each morning before heading to the
office. Adrienne wasn't angry or upset when she texted him. With
a smile on her face, she was lovingly nudging him to stay true to
his word. She was offering a gentle rebuke.

Greg was in a foul mood when he received the text. So this
is what he read: "Hey Greg, guess who forgot to make the bed
this morning? YOU. And guess who had to make it? ME. Greg,
we talked about chores for an ENTIRE HOUR on Saturday. Get
your act together and make the stupid bed."

Obviously, Greg misread her text.

What's the lesson here? It's not a good idea to rebuke your
spouse over text or email. Tone gets misinterpreted, body language is invisible, and the heart behind the rebuke is often hidden.

In Matthew 18:15, Jesus gives you an alternative approach for
rebuking your spouse. He tells you to "go" to your spouse and
speak face-to-face instead of hiding behind a screen and a key-
board. If you can't be in the same room, a video call is usually
just as good. If that's not possible, a phone call is your next best
option. Just don't type.

Why do we type instead of talk when we rebuke our spouses?
Here are three possibilities:

1. *We want control.* When we're typing, our spouses can't interrupt us. They can't talk over us. For a limited time, we can dictate the course of the conversation. We have control.
2. *We're impatient.* Sometimes face-to-face or phone chats have to wait for logistical reasons. But we want to vent our frustration *right now.* So we fire off texts or emails.
3. *We're lazy.* Typing out our frustrations takes less effort than engaging in potentially tumultuous and emotionally draining conversations.

Instead of typing, take an alternative approach when you rebuke your spouse. Don't text. Don't email.

Go to your spouse and talk.

Reflect as a Couple: How do you each feel when you receive an accusatory rebuke in written form from your spouse?

Reflect by Yourself: Why do you type instead of talk when you rebuke your spouse? What in your heart is driving this behavior? A desire for control? Impatience? Laziness? Impulsivity? Anger? Idolatry? Something else?

Act: Jesus Christ is the reason we rebuke our spouses face-to-face. He is in sovereign control over our conversations (Matt. 28:18), so we don't need to grasp after control by using our fingers instead of our voices. He has sent the Spirit to give us patience and self-control (Gal. 5:22–23), so we can hold off on our rebukes until we're with our spouses in person. Ultimately, in his infinite wisdom, he has commanded us to "go" to our spouses when we've been sinned against. If your spouse sins against you, obey Christ, honor your spouse, go, and talk.

DAY 13

Using Identity Statements

See what kind of love the Father has given to us, that we should be called children of God; and so we are. (1 John 3:1)

"YOU'RE DECEPTIVE. You're lazy. You're emotionally unstable. You're JUST LIKE YOUR MOTHER." Kevin hurled this onslaught of insults at his wife Erica during a recent fight. By the end, she was weeping—crushed by his accusations. Why were Kevin's insults so damaging?

They were identity statements.

What's an identity statement? It's an insult that puts a person in a box. You make an identity statement when you take a behavior, habit, character trait, physical attribute, or life event and define a person by it. You grossly label them based on something they've done, a quality they exude, how they look, or what they've experienced. All identity statements have one common element. They start with "You are _____."

Identity statements are destructive, demoralizing, and defeating. They have no place in conflict between two Christian spouses for one reason—they're untrue. You and your spouse are not your blunders, idiosyncrasies, appearances, or pasts. You are not your sins or shortcomings. You are not your faults or failures.

Who are you? *You are children of God* (1 John 3:1). You are beloved members of a holy family—the church—with Christ as its head (Eph. 5:23). And as members of this family, certain things hold true for you both. Here are just a few:

- *You are people in whom God has chosen to dwell.* Galatians 4:6 says that "God has sent the Spirit of his Son into our hearts, crying, 'Abba! Father!'"

- *You are rightful heirs to countless unfathomable and eternal spiritual blessings.* Romans 8:16–17 says, "The Spirit himself bears witness with our spirit that we are children of God, and if children, then heirs—heirs of God and fellow heirs with Christ."
- *You are free.* Galatians 4:7 says, "So you are no longer a slave, but a son." You are free from condemnation (Rom. 8:1). You are free from the power of sin (Rom. 6). You are free from the power of the devil (1 John 5:18). You are free from shame, fear, and guilt (Isa. 54:4; 2 Tim. 1:7; Heb. 8:12). You are no longer a slave. You. Are. Free.

You are children of God. You are deeply loved offspring of the Father—vessels in whom the Spirit lives, inheritors of glorious divine gifts, and spiritual siblings who have been freed from the grip of your flesh, the world, and the devil.

That's your identity. That's who you are.

Reflect as a Couple: How would a deep understanding of your shared identity as children of God change the way that you speak to each other when you're in conflict?

Reflect by Yourself: Who is your spouse? Take some time to write out an answer. Are you using God's words (Scripture) or your own words?

Act: To avoid identity statements, be as specific as possible when critiquing your spouse. For example, instead of saying, "You're worthless in the home," say, "You haven't been emptying the dishwasher each morning like you promised." Moving forward, grant each other permission to gently call out identity statements after they're made. If you make one, repent and restate your feedback in a constructive, specific, and loving manner.

DAY 14

Worshipping Your Spouse

And God spoke all these words, saying, "I am the LORD your God,
who brought you out of the land of Egypt, out of the house of slavery.
You shall have no other gods before me." (Exod. 20:1–3)

"I THINK I know why your marriage is falling apart. You're worshipping each other."

Evan and Lauren stared at me in confusion. They had been at each other's throats for an entire counseling session—screaming, crying, and swearing at each other. My statement made no sense to them. How were they worshipping each other? How had they turned each other into idols?

The answer lies in the definition of an idol. If you recall, on Day 1, I defined an idol as anything that we elevate above God in value, importance, power, and authority over our lives. Sadly, we turn our spouses into idols all the time when we're in conflict. We allow them to rule our minds, wills, and emotions. We let them dictate our thoughts, words, feelings, and reactions. We surrender our self-control on altars before them. We turn them into golden calves, hand over our hearts, and bow down to them.

And God isn't okay with it.

In Exodus 20:1–3, the first of the Ten Commandments, the Lord makes it clear that we are to worship him and him alone. How do you know if you're breaking this commandment and worshipping your spouse? Test yourself with the following questions:

- Is your marriage ruling your thought life?
- Does your spouse have an unhealthy grip on your emotions?
- Do you care more about what your spouse thinks of you than what God thinks of you?

- Do your spouse's words carry more weight than God's Word?

If your answer is yes to any of these, there's a good chance that your spouse has become an idol.

I'll admit that there's a fine line between holiness and idolatry in marriage. We're supposed to be mindful of our spouses but not allow them to consume our minds. We're supposed to be emotionally connected to them but not let them rule our emotions. We're supposed to care about what they think of us but not care *too* much. We're supposed to value their words but not more than God's. We're supposed to love our spouses but not love them more than Christ.

Yes, there's a fine line between matrimonial holiness and idolatry. If you stay on the right side of the line, it will bring life. If you cross it and worship your spouse, it will not only destroy you—it will destroy your marriage.

Reflect as a Couple: Are you worshipping each other as idols? If so, how?

Reflect by Yourself: Can you think of a specific problem area in your marriage that you think about way more than you think about God? Will you surrender this problem area into God's hands so you can focus more of your undivided attention on him?

Act: If you've turned your spouse into an idol, now is the time to confess this to God and ask for forgiveness. But it's also the time to rest in the fact that if you are a Christian, you are forgiven because of the sacrificial death of Jesus—the only person who walked this earth and never worshipped an idol. Move forward today in humble repentance for worshipping your spouse. Spend some dedicated time worshipping the only one who is truly worthy of your worship—Jesus Christ.

MARRIAGE CONFLICT
ESSENTIALS

DAY 15

Flee Temptation

No temptation has overtaken you that is not common to man.
God is faithful, and he will not let you be tempted beyond your
ability, but with the temptation he will also provide the way of
escape, that you may be able to endure it. (1 Cor. 10:13)

TUESDAY, 7:30 P.M. It's the worst time of the week for me to engage in a meaningful conversation with Abby. I've typically just walked through the door after eight back-to-back counseling sessions. My stomach is empty. My brain is fried. It's been at least thirteen hours since I've spent intentional time with God. I'm tempted to lash out at anybody who doesn't massage my back and feed me ice cream.

So what do I do at 7:30 p.m. on Tuesdays? I escape. I greet Abby and immediately go for a run. On my run, I listen to music that points me to Christ and resets my heart. In other words, I escape to God. I run out the door and run toward God before I have the chance to hurt my wife.

I base my Tuesday-night routine on 1 Corinthians 10:13. In the verse, Paul says at least two things. First, we all share the same set of temptations. We all have "Tuesday, 7:30 p.m." moments when we're tempted to hurt our spouses with our words. Five uniquely tempting situations are what I call the "DEATH states":

- *Drinking.* You've been consuming alcohol, and your inhibitions are low.
- *Exhausted.* Your body and mind are depleted. You need rest.
- *Angry.* You're agitated or annoyed at somebody or something.
- *Tense.* You're stressed and distracted by the worries of the world.

- *Hungry*. Your blood sugar is low, your body is frail, and your brain isn't working right.

If you're in a DEATH state, you will likely be tempted to verbally murder your spouse (Prov. 18:21).

But there's good news. In 1 Corinthians 10:13, Paul also says that God will provide a way of escape from any temptation. In other words, you don't *have* to verbally assault your spouse. While your escape route will depend on your unique personality and circumstances, your safest destination will always be the Lord. He is the one to whom you can and should always escape. You might escape to him through running and music like I do on Tuesday nights. You might escape to him through a gospel-centered conversation with a friend from church or through a time of focused prayer. Or you might do what Jesus did in Luke 4:1–13. In the midst of Satan's wilderness temptations, he escaped to God by going to Scripture. He directed his mind to the book of Deuteronomy and threw memorized verses in the devil's face. Eventually, Satan left him.

The Lord promises that we will be tempted to unleash wrath on our spouses. But he also promises a way out. Will you take it?

Reflect as a Couple: What are your respective "Tuesday, 7:30 p.m." moments? When are you most tempted to lash out at each other?

Reflect by Yourself: Do you believe that you are capable of withstanding any temptation by escaping to God?

Act: When only one of you is tempted to use ungodly speech, it's common for the other spouse to be offended if the tempted spouse "flees." Commit not to follow or antagonize your spouse when they need to flee. Instead, pray for them and ask when they will return.

DAY 16

Take Out the Log

"Why do you see the speck that is in your brother's eye, but do not notice the log that is in your own eye? . . . You hypocrite, first take the log out of your own eye, and then you will see clearly to take the speck out of your brother's eye." (Matt. 7:3, 5)

"YOU HAVE AN anger problem!"

With his blood boiling and his face red, Brian shouted these words at Carrie, his wife of fifteen years. They were in the middle of a contentious battle over where to spend the Christmas holiday—in Chicago with his family or in Iowa with hers. The discussion was civil at first, but at the five-minute mark it turned ugly. Each spouse accused the other of being selfish. Brian insulted Carrie's parents. Carrie returned the favor. Eventually, the conversation was nothing but yelling, slandering, blaming, and defending. When Brian could take no more, he stomped out of the room and slammed the door behind him. But before doing so, he screamed one final accusation: "You have an anger problem!" The hypocrisy was almost comical.

Sadly, we can be just as hypocritical as Brian in our own marriages. When conflict arises, we criticize our spouses for things that we also do. We accuse them of sins of which we are equally guilty—perhaps more guilty. We point out specks in their eyes when we have logs in our own.

How do we avoid such hypocrisy? Jesus gives us the answer in Matthew 7:3–5. There, he tells us to take the logs out of our eyes prior to calling out the specks in our spouses'. Before we address our spouses' shortcomings, we must humble ourselves, confess our sinful actions and sinful hearts, and turn to God in humble repentance.

Where do we get the humility and the courage necessary to admit that we have massive logs in our eyes? The gospel. The gospel says that two things are true of all Christians. First, we are infinitely sinful before an infinitely holy God (Rom. 3:23). We have more logs in our eyes than we could ever imagine. This should humble us. Second, God has forgiven us of every past, present, and future sin because Jesus Christ paid the penalty for them all on the cross. Knowing that our sins have been washed away by the blood of Jesus (1 John 1:7), we can be courageously transparent about our moral shortcomings.

The next time that you're tempted to criticize your spouse, press the pause button. Go into the bathroom. Look in the mirror. Find the log in your eye. Take it out. Then go and confess it to your spouse. Finally, lovingly and gently address the tiny little speck in your spouse's eye.

Reflect as a Couple: What makes it so hard to confess the logs in your eyes to each other? Pride? Self-righteousness? Fear? What can you each do to make confession safer in your marriage?

Reflect by Yourself: Do you have people from your local church whom you've granted permission to call out the specks in your eye? Have you put an accountability team in place to confront you on your sins and character flaws? Your spouse can't be the only person doing this.

Act: Are there unaddressed sins that your spouse has committed against you that are leading to bitterness or resentment in your heart? If so, tell your spouse. But only after first taking the log out of your own eye.

DAY 17

Change Your Glasses

*Finally, brothers, whatever is true, whatever is honorable,
whatever is just, whatever is pure, whatever is lovely, whatever
is commendable, if there is any excellence, if there is anything
worthy of praise, think about these things. (Phil. 4:8)*

I WROTE TODAY'S devotional on the final day of a long winter vacation with Abby. It wasn't the day that I expected. We were at her parents' brand-new home in southwest Florida. The plan was to spend the morning relaxing poolside, eat lunch at a gourmet lobster restaurant, and spend the afternoon celebrating her mom's birthday. We'd then head to the airport for a quick and easy direct flight home to New York City.

That all changed when I checked our flight status and learned that I had booked us on an 8 p.m. flight . . . *to Chicago*, not to New York City. Our only option was to rush to the airport for a 7:30 a.m. flight with a four-hour layover in St. Louis. We took it. And we paid an additional $500.

Our last day of vacation wouldn't be a day of fun but instead an expensive thirteen-hour travel day. Abby was devastated. So she left the room to take a walk and pray. When she returned ten minutes later, her words shocked me: "Thanks for taking the lead and checking on our flight, Steve. And thanks for being humble and apologizing. I appreciate it. Let's get going. We have a plane to catch!"

What did Abby do that morning? Exactly what Paul commands us to do in Philippians 4:8. There, he tells Christians to think about what is true, honorable, just, pure, lovely, commendable, excellent, and praiseworthy. He calls us to focus our minds on things of God, not on the brokenness of the world (or the stupidity of our spouses). That morning, instead of fixating on my absentmindedness, Abby chose to focus on my proactivity and humility. It changed the tone of the entire day.

Paul's counsel is critical when marriage conflict arises. It's easy to zero in on your spouse's mistakes, character flaws, and sins—to put on glasses through which you can see only the bad. But Paul says to take off those glasses and put on a pair through which you can see the God-given goodness in your spouse.

But what if there is *no* goodness in your spouse's attitude or behavior in the moment?

Then look beyond the moment. Focus on who your spouse *is* as a Christian—not on how they're acting right then and there. Focus your spouses' identity as a fellow member of Christ's body (Eph. 4:4), a temple of God's Spirit (1 Cor. 3:16), a beloved saint (Rom. 8:35–39; 1 Cor. 1:2), and a future citizen of heaven with you (Phil. 3:20). Focus on what *God* says about your spouse, not on how you feel about your spouse in that moment.

When your spouse sins against you, you don't have to stick your head in the sand and ignore the sin. But as you address it, put on a pair of Philippians 4:8 glasses. It will radically change your response.

Reflect as a Couple: Why is it so instinctive for each of you to focus on the bad instead of the good in your marriage?

Reflect by Yourself: How would wearing Philippians 4:8 glasses have impacted your last fight with your spouse?

Act: Spend fifteen minutes today writing out everything that is true, honorable, just, pure, lovely, commendable, excellent, and praiseworthy about your spouse.

DAY 18

Wear High Heels (or Air Jordans)

Rejoice with those who rejoice, weep with those who weep. (Rom. 12:15)

"Have you thought of hiring a cleaning lady?"

It was the worst thing that Tim could have said to his wife Beth. He had just gotten home after a long workday, and she was crying on the floor after twelve hours alone with their infant daughter and twin toddler boys. The baby was running a fever, refusing to eat, and screaming like a pterodactyl. The twins had been complaining, crying, and throwing regular tantrums all day. Beth usually cleaned the house during the kids' naps. The naps didn't happen. The cleaning didn't happen. So, with Beth sobbing on the floor, Tim suggested that they hire a cleaning lady.

Bad move.

Beth was emotionally reeling. What did Tim offer her? A solution. What did she need? Empathy. The most loving thing that Tim could have done was to sit down next to Beth, put his arm around her, listen to her cry, and speak her pain back to her in a way that showed that he understood how she was feeling.

The apostle Paul encourages us to show empathy in Romans 12:15, where he tells members of the Roman church to "rejoice with those who rejoice" and "weep with those who weep." I suspect that his command isn't limited to the emotions of joy and sorrow. In the context of marriage, he's instructing us to stretch ourselves to see the world through our spouses' eyes, walk in their shoes, and outwardly express their emotions back to them in a way that says, "I get you."

If empathy is hard for you, it will be especially difficult when conflict surfaces and emotions escalate. Here's a step-by-step process to help you to empathize in such situations:

- Consciously pause in the heat of the moment. Bite your tongue. Don't say anything.
- Take your eyes off yourself. Place them on your spouse.
- Ask your spouse how they're feeling in that moment (without sounding like a therapist).
- Work hard to internalize those feelings and make them your own. Get in your spouse's head. Embody their emotions.
- Verbalize those feelings back to your spouse in your own words.
- Ask if what you said accurately matches how they're feeling.

Why is empathy such a blessing to your spouse? It sends the message that their emotions are real, valid, and important. It tells your spouse that they're not a problem to be solved but instead a person to be known and loved. Most importantly, empathy models the incarnate and empathetic love of Christ—the one who chose to leave heaven, enter our world, feel our pain, truly know us, and die on our behalf.

It's critical to walk in your spouse's shoes in the midst of conflict. You might have to squeeze into high heels. You might have to clunk around in Air Jordans. It might be painful. It might be uncomfortable. But it will be worth it. I promise—your spouse will feel loved.

Reflect as a Couple: Is empathy exceptionally hard for either of you? Why? Why is it so important in marriage?

Reflect by Yourself: How do you feel when your spouse doesn't "get" you? That's how they feel when you don't "get" them.

Act: Begin a season of radical question-asking in your marriage. Commit to asking your spouse about their thoughts, emotions, victories, and struggles. Work hard to walk in your spouse's shoes and truly *know* them.

DAY 19

Customize Your Response

*And we urge you, brothers, admonish the idle, encourage the
faithhearted, help the weak, be patient with them all. (1 Thess. 5:14)*

"I THINK YOU'RE addicted to your job."

This was Carly's stinging rebuke of Ray when he called to tell
her that he would be working late. He was a high-level accountant
in the heart of tax season, and his boss had just informed his team
that they needed to work through the night. Having worked thirty
straight late nights, Ray was running on fumes. He was physically
ill from exhaustion. He missed Carly. He missed his kids. He
missed his bed. But he also knew that his choice was to say yes to
his boss or lose his job. So he conceded and called home with the
bad news. Carly proceeded to tell him that he was a workaholic.

Where did Carly go wrong? The answer lies in 1 Thessalonians 5:14. In this verse, Paul says that we need to calculate the
best way to respond to people in light of their unique spiritual,
emotional, and physical states. We should admonish the idle—a
term meaning "lazy" in Paul's immediate context but more gen-
erally referring to those who are habitually sinning. We should
encourage the fainthearted—those who are anxious, afraid,
depressed, discouraged, or emotionally exhausted. We should
help (physically serve) the weak—those who are suffering from
illness or injury and are unable to function without human aid.
In the case of Ray and Carly, Ray was fainthearted. He needed
encouragement. Carly gave him admonishment. Wrong move.

Need a model of how to live out 1 Thessalonians 5:14? Look
to Christ, the one who perfectly customized his treatment of the
sinful, fainthearted, and weak when he walked on earth. When
the sinful scribes and Pharisees were leading the people astray, he

slapped them with an entire Bible chapter full of admonishments (Matt. 23). When his disciples were fainthearted, he encouraged them by saying, "My peace I give to you. . . . Let not your hearts be troubled, neither let them be afraid" (John 14:27). When the weak—the blind, deaf, lame, and sick—begged him for healing, he graciously granted their requests (Matt. 11:5). Jesus modeled 1 Thessalonians 5:14 to a T.

It goes without saying that we are rarely *only* sinful, fainthearted, or weak. Your spouse will often be some combination of the three and will require a mixture of admonishment, encouragement, and physical help. But my charge to you today is to work hard to identify your spouse's *primary* need. Are they primarily in a state of sin, faintheartedness, or weakness? Adjust your approach accordingly.

Finally, when you admonish, encourage, or help your spouse, Paul also tells you to be patient with them. They are, as the verse implies, broken. They may not respond with gratitude. But rarely do you, I suspect, when our patient Lord offers you these very same gifts.

Reflect as a Couple: Which response (admonishment, encouragement, or help) do you each tend to use regardless of your spouse's condition? How is God calling you both to adjust to better follow 1 Thessalonians 5:14?

Reflect by Yourself: Can you think of a recent time when your approach toward your spouse didn't line up with their condition? How could you have responded differently?

Act: Share with each other the ways that you *like* to receive admonishment, encouragement, and help. Also share how you *don't* like to receive them. Alter the way that you admonish, encourage, and help each other accordingly.

DAY 20

Play Catch

Do you see a man who is hasty in his words? There is more hope for a fool than for him. (Prov. 29:20)

"STEVE, WHY DIDN'T you unload the dishwasher yesterday like you said you would?"

"Abby, why didn't you call the tax guy like you said *you* would?"

"Why are you changing the subject?"

"I'm not—I'm just saying that it isn't fair that you can forget something but I can't."

"Can you please just unload the dishwasher?"

"Can you please just show me a little grace?"

"Why are you being so defensive?"

"I'm not."

"You are. I hear it in your tone."

"No I'm *not*."

"Forget it. I'll unload the dishwasher myself."

Conversation complete. It took all of sixteen seconds.

No, this Sunday-afternoon Abby-Steve chat wasn't our finest moment as a couple. What was happening? First, I was being an infantile and condescending jerk. Second, we were playing "conversation ping-pong," violently swatting the conversation ball back and forth across the net of our living room. We weren't pausing to process each other's words. We weren't attempting to walk in each other's shoes. We certainly weren't reflecting on how we could best love each other in the midst of the conversation. We were firing comments and questions back and forth without digesting a word that the other was saying. We were playing ping-pong.

Conversation ping-pong is a deadly game. It sends the message that your spouse's words aren't important. But worse than this, it sends the message that *your spouse* isn't important.

In Proverbs 29:20, Solomon criticizes conversation ping-pong players. He says that one who is "hasty in his words" (a conversation ping-pong player) has less hope than a fool. He's doomed. If he's married, his marriage is doomed too.

Here's an alternative communication approach: *play catch.* Catch the conversation ball (listen to your spouse's words). Hold the ball for a little while (think about what your spouse just said). Finally, toss it back gently (speak in a loving manner). Listen. Think. Speak. In that order.

Playing catch is a slower, more calculated way to communicate. You must be willing to close your mouth and not interrupt—even when hurtful words are directed your way. How can you do this? Turn to Christ as both your model and your source of strength. Turn to the one who, like a lamb led to the slaughter, kept silent on his way to the cross instead of justifying himself (Isa. 53:7). Turn to the one who faced death and did not say a word in his defense. Turn to the one who didn't attack those who were attacking him, but instead laid down his life for them.

Conversation ping-pong is instinctual. But let me encourage you to put your paddle away and play some catch with your spouse.

Reflect as a Couple: When a conversation gets heated, is ping-pong your go-to game as a couple? If so, why?

Reflect by Yourself: What in your heart prevents you from playing catch with your spouse when conflict emerges?

Act: Practice playing catch the next time a conflict arises. Remember: listen, think, speak—in that order. It may feel unnatural at first. But with lots of practice, it will soon become instinctual.

DAY 21

Correct in Moderation

Good sense makes one slow to anger, and it is his glory to overlook an offense. (Prov. 19:11)

What If God Designed Marriage to Make Us Holy More Than to Make Us Happy?

It's the subtitle of Gary Thomas's best-selling book *Sacred Marriage*. I read the book on my honeymoon. Thomas's thesis was eye-opening: Abby wasn't there to make me happy, and I wasn't there to make her happy. Instead, the purpose of our marriage was to make us holy. As the Holy Spirit worked through us, we were to mold each other to look more like Jesus. We were to be instruments in God's hands to cleanse each other's polluted hearts, melt away each other's sinful habits, and prepare each other to meet Christ face-to-face in heaven.

Sadly, my approach to "sanctifying" Abby during our first year of marriage was utterly destructive. I corrected her incessantly. I pointed out her ungodly behavior, inappropriate speech, unhealthy emotions, and impure motivations as frequently and aggressively as possible. I'm surprised she didn't divorce me.

Why did I take this approach? First, I was spiritually and emotionally immature. Second, I was being a control freak. I was trying to micromanage Abby's path to holiness. Instead of trusting that God would purify her through the work of the Holy Spirit, I was trying to *be* the Holy Spirit. I was playing God and crushing Abby's heart in the process.

Proverbs 19:11 reminds us that it isn't our duty to point out every one of our spouses' faults, failures, or flaws. In fact, it is to our *glory* to overlook their offenses. No, this doesn't mean zipping our lips every time our spouses sin against us (Matt. 18:15). But it does mean frequently biting our tongues and entrusting their sanctification into God's hands instead of offering correction.

How do you know whether you should open or close your mouth when your spouse is falling short? There's no cookie-cutter answer, but here are a handful of helpful guidelines. Open your mouth if your spouse is

- being lazy, undisciplined, or irresponsible (1 Thess. 5:14);
- wandering from the faith (James 5:19–20);
- causing others to stumble (Mark 9:42);
- living in self-destructive rebellion against God (1 Tim. 5:20).

Otherwise, it might be best to close your mouth and overlook the offense.

It will be to your glory.

Reflect as a Couple: In what areas of your relationship have you been overly critical of each other? Where do you each need to be shown grace instead of criticism?

Reflect by Yourself: Why is it so hard to overlook your spouse's offenses?

Act: Verbal correction is not the only way to make your spouse holier. In fact, it should be the exception. A better approach to helping your spouse become more like Jesus is to model his character. Emulate him. *Show* your spouse how to be like Jesus—don't just tell them. With that said, try going one week without correcting, critiquing, or criticizing your spouse. Just one week. During that week, focus solely on emulating Christ with your character while entrusting your spouse's character into God's hands. See how it affects your interpersonal dynamic.

DAY 22

Always Build Up

Let no corrupting talk come out of your mouths, but only
such as is good for building up, as fits the occasion, that
it may give grace to those who hear. (Eph. 4:29)

DURING MY THIRD year at Gordon-Conwell Theological Seminary, I gave up crass humor for Lent. Ironically, I had developed a potty mouth during my time at the school. I was quoting off-color movies more than the Bible. I was telling crude jokes. I was making comments laced with tasteless sexual innuendo. My speech was sinful and hypocritical. People noticed—particularly my family. My brother even gave me the nickname "inappropriate seminary student."

Why was my speech so dirty during those seminary years? Part of me was trying to show the world that I could be a seminary student and still be "cool." Part of me was rebelling against the conservative Christian environment in which I was living and studying. Part of me wrongly thought that Christian freedom allowed me to be foul-mouthed. No matter the reason, I was demonstrating emotional, social, and spiritual immaturity with my verbal vulgarity.

So I made the decision to figuratively suck on a bar of soap during Lent. Nothing indecent, lowbrow, or profane would come from my mouth. No obscene jokes. No filthy movie references. Nothing offensive at all.

But was that good enough? No way. All I was doing during those forty days was committing not to say anything bad. But in Ephesians 4:29, Paul tells us that the holiness bar for our verbal communication should be much higher. Not only are we to eliminate all corrupting talk from our mouths, but every word that we say should *build up* those who are listening. One hundred percent of our speech is supposed to bless others.

In marriage, this means that we can't simply avoid saying hurtful things to our spouses and think that we're being good husbands or wives. We need to study our spouses and speak words that build them up. If they need correction, we should correct them. If they need to be reminded of God's promises, we should remind them. If they need to be encouraged, we should encourage them. No matter what gracious and edifying response they need, we should give it.

How do you know if you've passed the Ephesians 4:29 test after a conflict with your spouse? First, ask yourself if your words were unkind. But don't stop there. Second, ask yourself if you *built up* your spouse with your words. Ask if you showered your spouse with calculated grace. Ask if Christ would have spoken to your spouse in a similar manner.

Raise the bar. Always build up.

Reflect as a Couple: Has your standard for healthy communication been too low (not hurting each other)? Are you willing to raise the bar and begin a season in which you focus on building each other up with calculated, edifying words? It will take discipline. It will take humble reliance on the Spirit. Are you up for it?

Reflect by Yourself: Christ's body was broken (1 Cor. 11:24) to pay the penalty for your breaking down your spouse with your speech. Out of gratitude for this sacrifice, will you repent of your destructive words?

Act: Memorize the following modified version of Ephesians 4:29: "Let no corrupting talk come out of your mouth *in your marriage*, but only such as is good for building up [*spouse's name*], as fits the occasion, that it may give grace to [*spouse's name*]."

DAY 23

Rejoice When Criticized

The ear that listens to life-giving reproof will
dwell among the wise. (Prov. 15:31)

WHO IS THE wisest person you know? Perhaps it's a professor whose unmatched expertise leaves you in awe. Perhaps it's a pastor with an uncanny ability to relate Scripture to your unique life circumstances. Perhaps it's a counselor who always has the right thing to say to heal your bleeding heart.

How did this person become so wise? You may think their wisdom came as a result of education, age, or experience. It didn't. According to the book of Proverbs, the number one way that a person becomes wise is by hearing, internalizing, and applying constructive feedback (1:7; 8:33; 12:1; 13:1, 10; 15:5, 31; 19:20; 29:15). We grow in wisdom when we receive criticism with humble hearts and put it to good use.

If this is the case, then we have a remarkable opportunity to grow in wisdom in our marriages. After all, in what context are we criticized more?

Unfortunately, our spouses' "life-giving reproof" (Prov. 15:31) often goes to waste. We don't internalize it—let alone apply it. It beads off our hearts like water on a raincoat.

Why are we so quick to dismiss criticism from our spouses? Because it *really hurts*. Here's why:

- *It's often delivered in a not-so-gentle manner.* Unfortunately, in marriage, we take advantage of the security of the husband-wife relationship and let our guards down when we criticize. We speak without filters. We raise our voices. Our criticism comes across as derogatory, degrading, and disrespectful.

- *We know that our spouses' criticism is probably true.* Our husbands and wives have clear windows into our brokenness and sin. They know the truth about us—and the truth hurts.
- *We love our spouses.* We've given our hearts to our spouses. Naturally, we want them to love us back. When they criticize us, it feels like rejection from the person whose unconditional love we most desperately crave.

How do you move past the pain and rejoice when you're criticized by your spouse? You must fall in love with the prize: wisdom. The more you love wisdom, the more you will be willing to endure pain to get it.

But how do you fall in love with wisdom? For starters, don't try to fall in love with the concept of wisdom. Nobody can truly love a concept. Fall in love with wisdom personified. Meditate on the person and work of Christ and fall in love with the one whom Paul calls "the wisdom of God" (1 Cor. 1:24). The more you love Jesus, the more you will love wisdom. And the more you will rejoice when you are criticized by your spouse.

Reflect as a Couple: Does criticism breed animosity between the two of you? If so, why?

Reflect by Yourself: Is there valid criticism coming from your spouse right now that you are you stubbornly rejecting?

Act: The next time that you are criticized by your spouse, close your mouth, internalize the criticism, and ask yourself if there is even a *hint* of truth in it. If there is, repent of any pride that is keeping you from applying it, apply it, and thank God for making you wiser.

DAY 24

Accept Injustice

When he was reviled, he did not revile in return; when he suffered, he did not threaten, but continued entrusting himself to him who judges justly. (1 Peter 2:23)

"I'M TWO SECONDS away from leaving this office and never coming back." Kim made this threat to her husband Brent fifteen minutes into our first marriage counseling session. Brent had spent those initial fifteen minutes brutally attacking her from every angle. He blamed her for spending all their money. He accused her of manipulatively withholding sex. He insisted that it was her fault that their kids were acting out in school. Through an eclectic array of cutting accusations, he made it clear that *she* was the reason their family was falling apart. Not him.

But Brent's verbal onslaught, in and of itself, wasn't the reason Kim wanted out of the session. She wanted out because ninety percent of Brent's opening statement was untrue. He was lying, or at least exaggerating. His attacks were unjust, and she couldn't take it.

This happens often in marriage conflict. Your spouse falsely accuses you of wrongdoing. Your sins are exaggerated. Your good deeds are ignored. It isn't fair. Injustice abounds.

What do we do when our spouses treat us unjustly? Not surprisingly, we are called to emulate Christ. Peter tells us how to do so in 1 Peter 2:23. When the sinless, selfless Savior of the world was unjustly reviled, he did not revile in return. When the one who never should have suffered was taken to the cross, he did not fight back with threats, but instead focused on the Father who would one day justify him. Jesus willfully bore infinite injustice because he knew that he would eventually be vindicated by God.

Emulating Christ when your spouse acts unjustly means putting down your verbal weapons, refusing to hurt your spouse for their unjust behavior, and surrendering judgment into God's hands.

Three important disclaimers must be made:

- This verse isn't telling you to stay silent if there is physical, emotional, or spiritual abuse in your marriage. If you are being abused, please tell the proper authorities ASAP.
- This verse isn't telling you to be a doormat—to allow your spouse to habitually sin against you without addressing it (1 Thess. 5:14; see Day 19).
- This verse isn't telling you to give up your holy pursuit of justice for others. Where you see people suffering injustice, it is holy and pleasing to God for you to lovingly stand against it (Micah 6:8).

But 1 Peter 2:23 *is* telling you to take off your judge's robe when your spouse treats you unjustly. After all, the Father wore his at Calvary. And he will wear it again on judgment day (2 Peter 2:9).

Reflect as a Couple: Christ was punished on the cross for *all* the injustice in your marriage. How should this impact the way that you each respond when injustice comes your way?

Reflect by Yourself: How are you treating your spouse unjustly?

Act: Spend time praying together for two things: First, ask for the spiritual fruit of self-control (Gal. 5:23). Often, a lack of self-control causes us to lash out at our spouses when they treat us unjustly. Second, pray together for the ability to forebear, to forgive, and to entrust judgment into God's hands when you face injustice in your marriage.

DAY 25

Pay the Debt

*Then Peter came up and said to him, "Lord, how often will
my brother sin against me, and I forgive him? As many as
seven times?" Jesus said to him, "I do not say to you seven
times, but seventy-seven times." (Matt. 18:21–22)*

WHAT DOES IT mean to forgive a sin? I frequently ask couples
this question. More often than not, I get blank stares in return.

In Matthew 18:21–35, often called the "parable of the unforgiving servant," Jesus provides a clear definition of forgiveness. In
the story, a king forgives his servant an insane debt of two hundred thousand years' wages. That servant then finds a fellow servant who owes him a relatively tiny debt of one hundred days'
wages and demands that he pay him back. The king finds out. He's
infuriated. He scolds the unforgiving servant and sends him to
jail "until he should pay all his debt." In other words, he's never
getting out.

There's a lot to this parable, but today I want to highlight
the fact that Jesus equates sin with *debt*. When your spouse sins
against you, they incur a debt. They owe you something for the
pain that they've caused you. Forgiving your spouse, according to
Jesus, means doing two things.

First, it means releasing them from the debt. In other words,
it means not making your spouse pay for their sin. How could you
make them pay? You could punish them. You could belittle, mock,
or slander them. You could be passive-aggressive, condescending,
or rude toward them. If you're doing any of these, you're punishing your spouse and making them pay the debt.

Second, it means paying the debt yourself. Since a debt
can't just vanish into thin air, somebody has to pay it. When you

forgive your spouse, you're choosing to pay their debt—to willfully endure the pain that they deserve for sinning against you.

Here's what forgiveness looked like in two real-life marriages:

Hannah had a two-year affair with a coworker. She asked her husband Michael for forgiveness. He forgave her. He didn't punish Hannah for her sin, but instead took upon himself the pain that she deserved by willfully enduring heartache and grief.

In a recent rage episode, Ryan told Laura that he wished that he had never married her. He asked for forgiveness. Laura forgave him. She didn't punish Ryan for his sin, but instead took upon herself the pain that he deserved by willfully enduring sadness and shame.

How many times must we forgive our spouses? Jesus says seventy-seven times—a number symbolic of infinity. Is this difficult? Absolutely. But it's also liberating. In the same way that forgiving a financial debt breaks the enslaving chain between a borrower and a lender, so forgiving a sin breaks the enslaving chain between a sinner and the victim of their sin.

Forgiveness is hard. Paying your spouse's debt hurts.

But on the other side is freedom.

Reflect as a Couple: Are there areas of unforgiveness in your marriage?

Reflect by Yourself: Do you have a tough time forgiving? Why?

Act: Where do we get the ability to forgive "seventy-seven times"? The lesson from Matthew 18:21–35 is clear: the degree to which we understand the vertical forgiveness that we've received in Christ is the degree to which we will offer horizontal forgiveness to our spouses. Spend time together confessing the debts that you owe each other. After you're finished, take time to reflect on the forgiveness that you've both received in Christ. Finally, forgive each other.

DAY 26

Use *We*

If we say we have no sin, we deceive ourselves,
and the truth is not in us. (1 John 1:8)

OUT THE DOOR by four. Throwing up by ten.

This was Erin's experience at her brother-in-law's wedding. It was a big day for her husband Sean, as his oldest brother was finally tying the knot. Since Erin struggled with social anxiety, she was dreading the event. She hated large groups of people. She hated making small talk. She hated the pressure to be "on." To mitigate her anxiety, she had a couple of drinks before the ceremony, a couple more after the ceremony, a couple more during dinner, and a couple more during the reception. By nine o'clock she was drunk. By ten she was hurling in the hotel bathroom.

Sean was humiliated. The following evening, they sat down to talk about the wedding. Erin explained that she only drank because she was nervous. She was worried that she would have a panic attack in front of Sean's family. Sean's gentle response? "Then we have to find better ways to combat our anxiety. We can't turn to alcohol."

One word should stand out in Sean's subtle rebuke: *we*. It's a slight shift from the expected *you*. But it makes a huge difference. Using *we* when you correct your spouse sends two messages.

First, you are not morally superior. Using *we* says that you are no better than your spouse. You have plenty of sin in your heart as well (1 John 1:8). While you may not have committed the exact sin that your spouse just committed, chances are you've had similar unholy motives driving your unique sins.

Second, using *we* says that you are united. You are standing by your spouse, even after they've sinned. You remain united as one flesh (Eph. 5:31). You remain united as a brother and sister in Christ (John 1:12). You remain a united *we*.

Using *we* when admonishing your spouse isn't natural—especially if you're the victim of their sin. It requires extraordinary humility. How do you get this humility?

You can remember your own faults and failures. You can reflect on your mistakes and miscues. You can recall your slip-ups and sins. But you can't stop there. You must also stare at your Savior. You must set your eyes on the only person to whom 1 John 1:8 didn't apply—the one who didn't fall short of the glory of God but died as if he did. You must gaze at the innocent spouse (Rev. 19:7) who was crucified to pay the penalty for every sin that you've ever committed and ever will commit. You must focus on Jesus.

Using *we* when correcting your spouse takes humility, demonstrates humility, and humbles you. But most importantly, it exalts Christ—the one who "humbled himself by becoming obedient to the point of death, even death on a cross" (Phil 2:8).

Reflect as a Couple: Do you see yourselves as infinitely sinful relative to your infinitely holy Savior? How does this impact your ability to use *we* when you correct each other?

Reflect by Yourself: What in your heart resists using *we* when you admonish your spouse? Blindness to your sin? Blindness to your Savior?

Act: Spend ten minutes together in prayer, confessing (out loud) the ways that you have fallen short of God's glory in your marriage. As you do, use *we* instead of *I*.

DAY 27

Call a Time-Out If Necessary

But Jesus often withdrew to lonely places and prayed. (Luke 5:16 NIV)

"I'M IN A bad place. Let's press the pause button, take the day to pray, and talk after work."

It was the holiest thing that Abby could have said. She and I were bickering at the breakfast table one morning during our first month of marriage. Although we had less than five minutes to chat, I was foolishly trying to fit in a confrontational conversation about finances. My tone was insensitive and accusatory. Abby's was understandably angry and defensive. The tension in the room was rising. It was clear that we were on a one-way path to a blowout fight.

So Abby took a time-out. A twelve-hour time-out. Its purpose was twofold. First, it allowed us to reach a state of emotional equilibrium—a place where adrenaline was no longer tempting us to say things that we would later regret. Second, it allowed us to reach a state of spiritual clarity. For twelve hours, we could spend time with God and allow our thoughts to become his thoughts. In other words, Abby took the time-out to make sure that our healthiest and holiest selves would be having the conversation.

Where did Abby get the idea of a spiritual time-out? From Jesus. Today's verse says that he took them frequently—that he "often withdrew to lonely places and prayed." He made it a habit to remove himself from the world to align his heart with the Father's. He isolated himself with God to spiritually prepare himself for the confrontational and combative conversations to come. He stepped away—occasionally for entire nights (Luke 6:12)—to sit in the Father's love so he could pour out this love to others. In the end, Jesus took time-outs to worship the Father so he could effectively spur others to do the same.

We would do well to mirror Jesus and take time-outs when we're gridlocked in heated conversations with our spouses.

Here are three practical pointers for when you call a time-out in the midst of a conflict:

1. *Check your motives.* A time-out should never be used to punish your spouse or gain control. It's an opportunity for both of you to calm down and commune with Christ.
2. *State an explicit time when you will reconvene and continue the conversation.* I recommend limiting a time-out to one day.
3. *Be intentional with your time-out.* Pray, read Scripture, meditate, and spend time with other Christians (without gossiping). Don't let the time-out turn into a useless break in the conversation.

One last thing. You can't say no if your spouse requests a time-out. You must show self-control and walk away. It will be difficult, but it will honor both your spouse and God.

Time-outs. If Jesus took them, so should we.

Reflect as a Couple: Is it hard for each of you to request or concede to a time-out in the middle of a heated conversation? Why?

Reflect by Yourself: Jesus took one of his most famous time-outs in the garden of Gethsemane (Matt. 26:36–46). Why did he do so? What does this time-out teach you?

Act: Calling a time-out with a gentle and respectful tone is difficult when emotions are escalating during a conflict. For this reason, it might be wise to come up with a neutral "time-out signal." Pick one that works best for the two of you.

DAY 28

Pause and Pray

"If my people who are called by my name humble themselves, and pray and seek my face and turn from their wicked ways, then I will hear from heaven and will forgive their sin and heal their land." (2 Chron. 7:14)

SEVERAL MARRIAGE COUNSELING clients have called my methods a tad "unorthodox."

The statement is ironic, as I make every effort to ensure that my counseling methodology is rooted in orthodox Christianity. What my clients mean is that I do things a bit differently compared to other counselors. For example, I'm 100 percent willing to stop a combative marriage counseling session and ask each spouse to pray for the other out loud—right then and there. In all but a few cases, they've conceded to my request.

Why do I do this? My motivation is rooted in 2 Chronicles 7:14. In this verse, the Lord tells Solomon that if the Israelites will humble themselves, pray, seek his face, and turn from their wicked ways, he will, among other things, "heal their land." He will purify it and protect it from pests and drought.

What does Israel's land have to do with an angry couple?

If God promises to purify Israel's *land* should they turn to him in humility, prayer, and repentance, how much more will he purify two angry spouses' *hearts* should they turn to him in humility, prayer, and repentance? How much more will he eliminate the spiritual impurities (pests and drought) that are causing them to lash out against each other? How much more will he produce healthy fruit not from the ground but from the Spirit?

Practically speaking, what happens when you turn to Christ in prayer in the middle of a contentious verbal battle with your spouse? At least four things:

1. Prayer halts the back-and-forth ping-pong match (see Day 20) by redirecting the conversation vertically.
2. Prayer opens the door for the Holy Spirit to speak to each of you and convict you of the sins that you're committing in the conversation (John 16:8).
3. Prayer gives you a unique view into your spouse's heart. When you listen to your spouse talk humbly and vulnerably to God, you will hear beautiful words that you would not likely hear in any other context. When you hear these words, your heart toward your spouse will likely soften, and your ability to show compassion will likely grow.
4. Prayer helps you to collectively discern *God's* will—not yours—for the situation that you're arguing about.

Pray together. Pray in times of peace. But perhaps more importantly, pray in times of conflict. Right then and there.

Reflect as a Couple: Is it a common practice for you to pray as a couple? If not, why not?

Reflect by Yourself: When Jesus Christ was being crucified on the cross, he prayed, "Father, forgive them, for they know not what they do" (Luke 23:34). If Christ could stop and pray for those murdering him while in the middle of the "conflict" of his crucifixion, you can stop and pray for your spouse in the middle of your marriage conflict.

Act: If you don't pray together regularly, chances are small that you will pray together when conflict arises. Starting today— yes, today—commit to spending fifteen minutes a day praying together. Establish a set time and place that minimizes distractions.

MARRIAGE CONFLICT
AND COMMUNITY

DAY 29

Be Golden When Talking to Others

"And as you wish that others would do to you, do so to them." (Luke 6:31)

THE GOLDEN RULE.

Do to others as you would have them do to you. You probably learned it as a child. Most world religions teach it. Even most atheists agree with it. It's the closest thing that our world has to a universal moral code. We should treat others how we would want to be treated.

The Bible presents its version of the Golden Rule in Luke 6:31. Jesus places the command in the middle of a lesson on how to love our enemies (Luke 6:27–36). We love them well by treating them how we would want to be treated.

The Golden Rule is critical when we're engaging in intense, face-to-face conflicts with our spouses—when we're arguing in real time and they feel like our enemies. We should treat them as we would want to be treated. But following it is just as important when we're *away* from them—when we're removed from the conflict and are tempted to bad-mouth, berate, slander, or smear them in front of others. The Golden Rule says that we must speak about our spouses as we would want them to speak about us. This doesn't mean simply avoiding gossip. It means *building up* our spouses to others (Eph. 4:29; see Day 22). It means describing them with words of dignity and deference. It means showcasing their strengths instead of highlighting their weaknesses. It means displaying them to the world in a way that would make them smile if they were eavesdropping.

I'm not insisting that you put on a happy mask and embellish how wonderful your spouse is when the two of you are in a rough patch. The goal isn't to be fake. I'm simply asking you to present your spouse to others with a heart of love and respect (Eph. 5:32–33)—to speak about them as Christ would speak about them.

And as my mom said to me growing up, "If you don't have anything nice to say, don't say anything at all."

The question begs to be asked: how is the Golden Rule of Christianity different from the Golden Rule of other world religions and the version followed by atheists? It boils down to the motivation behind it. As Christians, we don't follow the Golden Rule out of shallow sentimentality or moralistic good will. We follow it to honor and obey Jesus—the only one who has ever followed the Golden Rule perfectly. We follow it out of gratitude that he lovingly laid down his life for us even though we constantly break the Golden Rule. We don't follow the Golden Rule to become "golden" in God's eyes—we follow it out of thanksgiving that we're already golden in his eyes because of Christ's work on the cross.

With these godly motivations, commit today to speak well about your spouse to others, even—no, *especially*—when you're in conflict.

Reflect as a Couple: Why is it so important not to slander each other when you're in conflict? What possible collateral damage could result?

Reflect by Yourself: Do you gossip about your spouse? Will you put an end to it?

Act: Barring situations in which abuse is taking place in the marriage, it's always good to tell your spouse when you're going to speak about your marriage struggles with others. Assuming that your spouse is supportive of you sharing with these people, make sure to speak words that would delight your spouse if they were in the room.

DAY 30

Consult Relatives Selectively

*Therefore a man shall leave his father and his mother and hold
fast to his wife, and they shall become one flesh. (Gen. 2:24)*

"MY PARENTS AGREE that you drink too much."

When Matt heard this, it felt like a knife in his back. He and
his wife Angela were in the middle of a tense marriage counseling
session and the topic of his drinking came up. Angela revealed
that she had spoken to her parents and aired their—more specifically *his*—dirty laundry. Matt felt that she had sinned against him
by doing so.

He was right. Genesis 2:24 tells us why. In this verse, the
author says that a man and a woman do two things when they
get married. First, they "leave" their parents. In fact, they leave all
members of their immediate families. Second, they become "one
flesh." They join a brand-new immediate family consisting of two
members who are so tightly bonded that their metaphorical skin
fuses together. When Angela gossiped about Matt to her mom,
she had not left her parents. In reality, she was momentarily leaving Matt. This was her sin.

But sin isn't the only issue here. I'd also argue that it's *unwise*
to share marriage difficulties with your relatives. Allow me to provide three reasons why.

First, relatives are often bad counselors. Unless your relatives
have substantial spiritual and emotional maturity, they will likely
take your side. And your spouse's relatives will likely take your
spouse's side. In other words, relatives are biased. And biased
counselors rarely provide good counsel.

Second, lasting impressions may result. If you speak ill of your
spouse to your relatives, the lens through which they view your

spouse will darken. If you share enough dirt, you can make this lens opaque—blocking their ability to see any good in your spouse.

Third, relational triangles may form. A relational triangle occurs when two people are pitted against a third, leaving the third person feeling attacked and isolated. When you share your marriage struggles with relatives, you run the risk of forming relational triangles, leaving your spouse feeling like an outcast in the family.

If, in exceptional circumstances, the two of you agree to consult a relative when you're in conflict, may I provide two quick tips? First, make sure that you're both present during the conversation. You want to be on the same page regarding what was shared. Second, never belittle your spouse in front of your relatives. Speak well of them as you discuss the conflict.

Hear me: I'm not telling you to sever your extended-family relationships because you've tied the knot. I want you and your relatives to continue forming and sustaining meaningful, life-long, life-giving bonds. I'm simply challenging you to think twice before turning to them with your marriage problems. It could tear your one flesh apart.

Reflect as a Couple: Have you both truly "left" your parents and become one flesh? If not, what needs to happen to obey Genesis 2:24?

Reflect by Yourself: Have you slandered your spouse to your family in the past? Will you stop?

Act: Because Jesus Christ left his parent (the Father) to lay down his life for his bride (the church), you can joyfully leave your parents (and all your relatives) and lay down your life for your spouse. If you haven't left your relatives, do so today. With kindness, gentleness, and language that they will understand, explain the boundaries that you need to put in place to protect your marriage and honor God.

DAY 31

Call In the Reserves

Where there is no guidance, a people falls, but in an
abundance of counselors there is safety. (Prov. 11:14)

ABBY AND I were in marriage counseling when I was a marriage counselor in Washington, DC.

Our marriage wasn't crumbling. We weren't on the brink of divorce. We simply needed to work through a few complicated issues and weren't finding success resolving them on our own. So we called on a trusted Christ-centered counselor for help.

You might find this ironic, if not hypocritical. After all, shouldn't I, an "expert" on marriage (ha!), have the most polished of marriages? And if Abby and I were somehow having problems, shouldn't I have been able to fix them without calling on another counselor?

Yeah right. All marriages consist of two conflict-prone sinners who need Christ-centered counselors—even if they themselves are Christ-centered counselors.

Solomon backs me up in Proverbs 11:14. While he's using military language, his message also applies to marriage. In this proverb, we learn at least two things.

First, if you and your spouse ("a people") try to resolve your conflicts without guidance, you will "fall." Your weak marital legs won't be able to withstand the vicious attacks of your enemies—the world, your flesh, and the devil. Your one-flesh body will collapse.

Second, there's a way to avoid defeat when conflict arises. Solomon says to surround yourselves with "an abundance of counselors." In your case, I suggest a team of counselors that includes your pastor, a trusted elder, a spiritually mature married couple in your church, and, if necessary, a formal Christ-centered marriage counselor. This team of counselors can provide at least four services:

1. *Sin exposure.* Counselors can point out sins to which you are blind while gracefully leading you to life-giving repentance.
2. *Communication commentary.* Counselors can see and call out poor communication habits in real time as they watch the two of you talk together.
3. *Accountability.* Godly third parties in the room will hopefully keep you on your best behavior, enabling you to have healthier, holier, and more productive conversations.
4. *Objective advice.* Unlike family members, your team of counselors will hopefully lack bias. They can provide impartial advice and point you to relevant Scriptures instead of showering you with skewed opinions.

If your relationship is on the rocks, bring an abundance of counselors into your marriage. If you're doing okay but need to work through a nagging conflict, bring an abundance of counselors into your marriage. If your marriage is thriving, you should still bring an abundance of counselors into your marriage. Doing so will only strengthen you to achieve victory when the enemies attack.

Reflect as a Couple: Who are the formal or informal Christ-centered counselors helping the two of you in your marriage? Do you have an abundance of them? If not, why not?

Reflect by Yourself: Are you resistant to bringing others into your marriage? If so, why?

Act: Christian counseling isn't Christian if it isn't centered on Christ. If you bring counselors into your marriage, make sure they are not merely professing Christians offering secular counsel. Make sure that both their methods and words are Christ-centered.

CONCLUSION

In All Things, Love

You've made it.

You've shown perseverance, discipline, and commitment and have completed this challenging thirty-one-day marriage devotional. You've worked hard on your own. You've worked hard with your spouse. You've worked hard with God. You should be commended for your hard work. Well done, good and faithful servant.

I'd like to conclude this devotional by giving you two parting exhortations. I promise that if you follow through on them, your marriage will thrive. And I promise that if you don't, your marriage will struggle. Both exhortations are different versions of the same command:

Love.

First, *love your spouse* when you're in conflict. Sounds simple, right? It's not. It's really hard. Really, really hard. The form of love that I'm encouraging you to show is what I call "1 Corinthians 13 love," based on 1 Corinthians 13:4–7, a passage frequently read in wedding ceremonies yet rarely practiced in real-life marriages:

> Love is patient and kind; love does not envy or boast; it is not arrogant or rude. It does not insist on its own way; it is not irritable or resentful; it does not rejoice at wrongdoing, but rejoices with the truth. Love bears all things, believes all things, hopes all things, endures all things.

Showing 1 Corinthians 13 love when you're in conflict means being patient, kind, and humble toward your spouse when impatience, judgment, and pride are far more instinctive and far more pleasurable. It means emptying yourself—with God's help—of

envy, rudeness, irritability, resentment, wickedness, and deception. It means bearing your spouse's burdens, speaking faith-
infusing words, and offering hope when life feels hopeless. Ultimately, showing 1 Corinthians 13 love means showing Christ's
love to your spouse.

How do you gain the ability to show your spouse this 1 Corinthians 13 love in the midst of conflict? The answer lies in my second parting exhortation: *love Christ*. The more you love Christ,
the more you will show your spouse 1 Corinthians 13 love. The
logic goes like this. As you actively, consistently, and fervently
pour love into Christ, your heart will attach to him (Matt. 6:21).
As your heart attaches to Christ, you will start to mirror him. You
will begin to think, speak, and act like him. You will love others
like he loves them. Specifically, you will love your spouse like he
loves your spouse—with 1 Corinthians 13 love.

But let's get practical. How do you love Christ? Let me give
you ten ways to do so—a closing "What do we do now?" list:

1. *Love Christ by obeying him.* John 14:15 says, "If you love me,
   you will keep my commandments." You can show Christ love
   by adhering to his loving commands articulated in Scripture—commands that, if followed, will result in unmatchable
   joy, contentment, and peace.
2. *Love Christ with your time.* Start your day by spending time
   with Jesus. End your day by spending time with Jesus.
   Between these bookends, spend spurts of free time delight-
   ing in your Savior. Give him the treasure of your time.
3. *Love Christ with your energy.* Serve at your local church.
   Perhaps it's time for you to lead or host a small group. Perhaps you can volunteer on the Sunday service set-up team.
   Depending on your age and experience, perhaps you can
   mentor a younger couple. The list of ways to love Christ with
   your energy is endless. Don't burn yourself out, but also don't
   sit on the sidelines.

4. *Love Christ by telling others about him.* Jesus wants you to talk about him. Tell people about the hope that is in you (1 Peter 3:15). Tell people how Christ has changed your life. Tell people how he can change their lives. Share the gospel with people as frequently and joyfully as possible.

5. *Love Christ with your money.* Give your money away generously. Give to your local church. Give to parachurch ministries. Give spontaneously to those in need. Use wisdom in your giving, but give extravagantly.

6. *Love Christ by learning about him.* You can't love somebody you don't know. Where can you learn about Jesus? The Bible. May I suggest beginning a one-year Bible-reading plan? Structure is often helpful when it comes to consistent Bible reading. Also, memorize Scripture so it can be on the tip of your tongue at all times (Josh. 1:8).

7. *Love Christ by talking to him.* Pray without ceasing (1 Thess. 5:17). Make Jesus your go-to conversation partner. He wants to hear from you. Talk to him.

8. *Love Christ by loving other Christians.* Again, immerse yourself in your local church and love other Christians sacrificially in the context of the fellowship of believers.

9. *Love Christ by loving the lost.* Christ loved you and died for you while you were his enemy (Rom. 5:8). Lovingly emulate your Savior by loving those who reject him. Be kind and gentle toward your coworkers and neighbors who aren't Christians. Humbly serve your unbelieving friends and family. Love those who hate Christ.

10. *Love Christ by worshipping him.* Everything you do should be an act of worship directed toward your loving Redeemer. Worship him in your work. Worship him as you exercise. Worship him as you cook, clean, and take care of your family. Worship should not be limited to Sunday services.

If you do these things—if you pour love into Christ—I trust that your heart will attach to him, your mind will think like his, your actions will emulate his, and your love toward your spouse will mirror his 1 Corinthians 13 love.

Most wedding ceremonies mention 1 Corinthians 13:4–7. It's time to live it out in your marriage. With that said, I'd like to close this thirty-one-day journey in the same way that I started it—with a simple prayer for you:

> Lord Jesus, may you shower this couple with your 1 Corinthians 13 love. May this love permeate their hearts and change them inside and out. May it guide them as they navigate the seemingly impossible challenges of marriage. May it dictate the way that they communicate in the midst of conflict. And may you receive all the honor, glory, and praise as a result.
>
> In your holy name I pray. Amen.

Acknowledgments

THANK YOU, DEEPAK, for believing in me and for giving me the chance to contribute to this important series.

Thank you, Ed, for your Christ-centered counsel and your Christ-centered heart.

Thank you, Tim and Kathy, for teaching me the meaning of marriage.

Thank you, Bill and Mindy, for modeling what a godly marriage looks like in real life.

Thank you, Momma, for your words of wisdom while I wrote this devotional.

And last, but certainly not least, a special thank-you to my wife Abby. Thank you for putting up with me with such grace, patience, and kindness. Thank you for goofing around with me and making me laugh every day that we're together. Thank you for encouraging me, praying with me, and continually pointing me to Jesus. Thank you for being my biggest fan. Thank you for being my best friend. Thank you for being . . . you.

Suggested Resources for the Journey Together

Books

Keller, Timothy, with Kathy Keller. *The Meaning of Marriage: Facing the Complexities of Commitment with the Wisdom of God.* New York: Dutton, 2011. [The gold standard of marriage books. It also contains a study guide: Timothy Keller, Kathy Keller, and Spence Shelton, *The Meaning of Marriage: A Vision for Married and Single People* (Grand Rapids: Zondervan, 2015)—a six-session complement to the main book, which is available as a book and as a separate accompanying DVD.]

Lane, Timothy S., and Paul David Tripp. *How People Change.* Greensboro, NC: New Growth Press, 2006. [While this book is not specifically about marriage conflict, it eloquently describes the process of how our hearts become holier. As our hearts become holier, so will the way that we engage in marriage conflict.]

Priolo, Lou. *Resolving Conflict: How to Make, Disturb, and Keep Peace.* Phillipsburg, NJ: P&R Publishing, 2016. [A helpful analysis of the nature of conflict and how necessary it is if we are to live in true peace with one another. Filled with practical tools for healthy conflict resolution.]

Sande, Ken, and Kevin Johnson. *Resolving Everyday Conflict.* Updated ed. Grand Rapids: Baker Books, 2015. [A concise and biblical guide to peacemaking in everyday tumultuous relationships.]

Tripp, Paul David. *War of Words: Getting to the Heart of Your Communication Struggles.* Phillipsburg, NJ: P&R Publishing, 2000. [A big-picture book that reminds us how faith in the gospel of Jesus Christ transforms the way that we communicate.]

Articles and Booklets

Lane, Timothy S. *Conflict: A Redemptive Opportunity*. Greensboro, NC: New Growth Press, 2009. [A short, practical booklet that provides useful biblical principles to help you to grow through conflict.]

Powlison, David. "X-ray Questions: Drawing Out the Whys and Wherefores of Human Behavior." *The Journal of Biblical Counseling* 18, no. 1 (1999): 2–9. [An insightful article that pushes you to dig to the roots of why you say what you say and do what you do. The article is particularly helpful for identifying the heart problems that cause ungodly communication during marriage conflict.]

BIBLICAL
COUNSELING
COALITION

The Biblical Counseling Coalition (BCC) is passionate about enhancing and advancing biblical counseling globally. We accomplish this through broadcasting, connecting, and collaborating.

Broadcasting promotes gospel-centered biblical counseling ministries and resources to bring hope and healing to hurting people around the world. We promote biblical counseling in a number of ways: through our *15:14* podcast, website (biblicalcounselingcoalition.org), partner ministry, conference attendance, and personal relationships.

Connecting biblical counselors and biblical counseling ministries is a central component of the BCC. The BCC was founded by leaders in the biblical counseling movement who saw the need for and the power behind building a strong global network of biblical counselors. We introduce individuals and ministries to one another to establish gospel-centered relationships.

Collaboration is the natural outgrowth of our connecting efforts. We truly believe that biblical counselors and ministries can accomplish more by working together. The BCC Confessional Statement, which is a clear and comprehensive definition of biblical counseling, was created through the cooperative effort of over thirty leading biblical counselors. The BCC has also published a three-part series of multi-contributor works that bring theological wisdom and practical expertise to pastors, church leaders, counseling practitioners, and students. Each year we are able to facilitate the production of numerous resources, including books, articles, videos, audio resources, and a host of other helps for biblical counselors. Working together allows us to provide robust resources and develop best practices in biblical counseling so that we can hone the ministry of soul care in the church.

To learn more about the BCC, visit biblicalcounselingcoalition.org.

More Marriage Resources from P&R Publishing

For better . . . or for worse?

Whichever term describes your marriage, there are ways to make it (even) better. That's because God has designed marriage to be a relationship of deep unity and strength. Despite the challenges that couples face today, marital harmony need not be considered an impossible ideal.

Wayne A. Mack recognizes the challenges before us and shows us how to meet those challenges with growing success. In this book, he has gathered a wealth of biblical insight and practical information on marital roles, communication, finances, sex, child-rearing, and family worship. Both as a counseling aid and as a guide for husbands and wives to study together, this book offers true hope and help where couples need it most.

More Marriage Resources from P&R Publishing

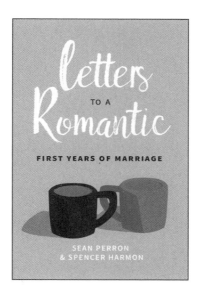

In warm, short, practical letters, Sean and Spencer guide couples through some common "firsts"—from major choices like deciding when to start a family, to the everyday details of establishing holy household habits, to the concerns raised by common sexual issues in marriage. You will discover the biblical wisdom you need to lay a foundation for a healthy and God-honoring lifelong relationship.

"A remarkable resource. It manages to be both extremely practical and persistently gospel focused. . . . Whether you consider yourself a 'romantic' or not, this book will strengthen every young marriage . . . and I can personally report that their wisdom is strengthening at least one older marriage too!"
    —**Alasdair Groves**, Executive Director, Christian Counseling and Educational Foundation

More Marriage Resources from P&R Publishing

Written both for newlyweds and for those who have long been married, this biblical, practical book helps couples to restore warmth and vitality to their marriages.

"*Sweethearts for a Lifetime* roots marriage in Christ and the gospel, and in separate sections devoted to men and women it identifies the callings God has clearly given them in Scripture. This book bears reading and rereading by couples together!"
   —**Tedd Tripp**, Pastor, Author, Conference Speaker

"Christian marriages are meant to get better over time. It is for want of knowing and applying the truths Wayne Mack has spelled out so well in this book that many marriages do not."
   —**Martin Holdt**, Pastor, Constantia Park Baptist Church

Was this book helpful to you?
Consider writing a review online.
The author appreciates your feedback!

Or write to P&R at editorial@prpbooks.com
with your comments. We'd love to hear from you.